Essential Elements of
Effective Discipline

Essential Elements of Effective Discipline

C. M. Charles
San Diego State University

Allyn and Bacon

Boston ▪ London ▪ Toronto ▪ Sydney ▪ Tokyo ▪ Singapore

Series Editor: *Arnis E. Burvikovs*
Editorial Assistant: *Matthew Forster*
Marketing Manager: *Amy Cronin*
Editorial–Production Administrator: *Michael A. Granger*
Editorial–Production Service: *Chestnut Hill Enterprises, Inc.*
Composition and Prepress Buyer: *Linda Cox*
Manufacturing Buyer: *Julie McNeill*
Cover Administrator: *Kristina Mose-Libon*
Electronic Composition: *Omegatype Typography, Inc.*

Library of Congress Cataloging-in-Publication Data
Charles, C. M.
    Essential elements of effective discipline / C. M. Charles
        p. cm.
    Includes bibliographical references (p.) and index.
    ISBN 0-201-72948-2
    1. School discipline. 2. Behavior modification. 3. Teacher-student relationships. I.
Title.

    LB3012.C47 2002
    371.102'4—dc21

2001053766

Printed in the United States of America

10 9 8 7 6 5 4 3 2 1   06 05 04 03 02 01

CONTENTS

16   In Review: The Nature and Procedures of Helpful Discipline   97

PART ONE

Facing the Discipline Problem

Part 1 reviews the discipline problem that is damaging education everywhere and identifies reasons for the problem and its persistence. A proposed solution, called Helpful Discipline, is introduced. Following that, a group of tasks is described that enable one to implement Helpful Discipline. The first task is then described. It entails examining faulty concepts of discipline and replacing them with more accurate ones.

CHAPTER

1 The Discipline Problem and Its Solution

This chapter reviews the damage that student misbehavior is doing to education everywhere and suggests a procedure for resolving the problem. The components of an effective system of discipline—Helpful Discipline—are introduced.

How Misbehavior Is Harming Education

Our schools are in the grip of a serious problem that is wreaking havoc on teaching and learning. That problem is student misbehavior. If you are now teaching, you have had ample experience with it. If you are preparing to teach, be forewarned: It is the major obstacle to your success and has the potential to destroy your career.

Misbehavior, often called "poor discipline," is the constant bane of teachers, not only in the United States but around the world. In milder cases of misbehavior, Julian constantly talks out during lessons and Alicia gazes out the window instead of working. In more worrisome cases, Janice disrespectfully talks back to the teacher at every opportunity, and Tony aggressively bullies other students. Any teacher would have difficulty dealing with these conditions on a daily basis. But imagine what a burden it is for teachers who must continually deal with students who, it would appear, despise school, have little sense of ethics and responsibility, and see nothing wrong with making teachers' lives miserable. The number of such students is increasing steadily and, because of that, many teachers are leaving education for greener pastures.

We mustn't tar all students with the bad discipline brush. A majority still shows good intentions and willingness to cooperate, and many bring great pleasure to teachers' lives. But the inescapable fact is a growing number misbehave so badly they spoil learning for everyone around them. Teachers complain of the frustration and stress this produces, which harms them psychologically and physically, removes satisfaction from teaching, and ruins their performance.

It's not just teachers who suffer. Students fail to reach levels of learning they should easily attain, and many of them become alienated from school. You can see that misbehavior is shortchanging everyone—students, teachers, parents, society, and taxpayers. The situation seems irreparable and entrenched. Numbers of teachers have lost hope that it will ever get better, yet the problem is not insoluble. To the contrary, it can be corrected rather easily in a short amount of time. This statement is so contrary to what most teachers believe that they have a hard time accepting it. But the proof is in the pudding, as you will see.

Why the Discipline Problem Persists

The Phi Delta Kappa Gallup Polls conducted over the past 30 years (see Elam, Rose, & Gallup, 2000) show that, despite widespread efforts to deal with misbehavior, the discipline problem is as serious as ever, certainly more serious than it was a few decades ago. One wonders why it hangs on so persistently, especially when nobody wants it—not teachers, parents, administrators, the public, or even the students. It is almost as if misbehavior has a life of its own. The reasons behind its persistence are numerous, and many of them are beyond educators' reach. But we can deal with the majority of them, especially those that originate in students, learning environments, and school personnel.

If you wish to counter this problem in your classes, look into the causes of misbehavior. This will permit you to see which causes you can deal with, and how. As you examine the causes, you will see that some can be eliminated entirely. Those that can't be eliminated can be modified or avoided. The causes seem to lie in five realms: (1) the fabric of society, (2) individual students' psyches, (3) class groups, (4) instructional environments, and (5) the adult personnel who work with students.

We can't do much about causes that lie within the larger society, except to recognize their existence and effects, discuss them with students, and work around them as much as possible. Examples of societal causes are decline in respect for authority and erosion of ethical consciousness.

We can, however, deal quite effectively with causes that reside in individual students, class groups, learning environments, and school personnel. Examples of causes that originate in individual students are egocentrism and inappropriate habits. Examples that originate in peer groups include provocation and group influence. Examples that originate in instructional environments are tedium and meaninglessness. Examples that originate in school personnel are poor modeling and poor communication. Chapters 10 and 11 explain how to address these problems. As you correct or ameliorate them, you simultaneously teach students that humane, considerate behavior serves them better than does boorish, inconsiderate behavior, and that the school experience can be enjoyable rather than disagreeable.

What All Teachers Want and Need

Teachers want students to learn, behave civilly in the classroom, and enjoy themselves while doing so. Seldom does anyone tell teachers they need—and are entitled—to enjoy their work and have a sense of accomplishment, too. We have learned that in today's schools we cannot *make* those things happen by scolding, reprimanding, coercing, forcing, punishing, bribing, or making demands. When we use such tactics, the results are invariably disappointing in a number of ways, as we shall see later.

Educators have long needed an alternative approach to discipline that is truly effective and that brings the results we desire without damaging feelings, relationships, or motivation to learn. Such an approach is now available and can be implemented easily.

The Solution Set Forth in This Book

The pages that follow describe a highly effective approach to class discipline that is based on helpfulness rather than coercion. It is called Helpful Discipline. Please take a moment to preview its rationale, its fundamental quality of helpfulness, what it can accomplish, and the components that comprise it.

Rationale for Helpful Discipline

Discipline is what we do to help students behave appropriately in school. Many of the discipline techniques we have relied on are ineffective, especially those that involve demanding, bossing, scolding, warning, belittling, and punishing. Those tactics can keep behavior partially under control for a while, but they do not last long. Worse, they produce detrimental side effects that inhibit learning, such as uneasiness, fearfulness, evasiveness, avoidance, dishonesty, undesirable attitudes toward learning, overall dislike for school and teachers, inclination to retaliate, and, for many, the desire to leave school as soon as possible. Discipline that produces those results cannot be called effective. Truly effective discipline helps students behave appropriately while maintaining good relations and willingness to cooperate.

What Helpful Discipline Accomplishes

Helpful Discipline uses no force, intimidation, or belittlement. It never tries to "make" students do anything. Yet it powerfully accomplishes the following:

- helps students progress strongly toward the goals of education, including significant learning, positive attitudes, responsibility, and self-direction;
- helps students relinquish self-defeating behavior in favor of positive behavior that brings success in school;
- maintains positive relationships among students and between the teacher and students;
- promotes a strong sense of personal dignity;
- develops student self-control and the ability to resolve conflicts productively;
- strengthens personal character and the character of the class as a whole.

The Quality of Helpfulness

Helpfulness is the fundamental quality of effective discipline. Students respond to it positively and it takes away most incentives to misbehave. There are certain exceptions, of course. Some students in special education and some in classes for the difficult to control sometimes require behavior modification and even more stringent methods of behavior management. But, for almost all students in almost all schools, helpfulness is the most effective strategy. It attunes teachers' and students' minds to student success in school and encourages them to work together to achieve it.

In Helpful Discipline, we never try to make students behave properly. Instead, we help them see the advantage of doing so, through good modeling, inspiration, encouragement, and close collaboration in decisions that affect the class. When we do those things—and many others that will be explained later—students quickly begin to behave appropriately because it seems to them the natural thing to do.

Most teachers would love to teach this way, but are afraid that, if they do, they will lose control completely. For the time being, open your mind to the possibility that the opposite will occur, that a gentle helpful approach, properly used, will eliminate most misbehavior, make students more cooperative, and lead to stronger learning and more positive attitudes. The purpose of this book is to show you how that is done.

Components of Helpful Discipline

The special value of helpfulness was pointed out many years ago by psychologist Haim Ginott (1972). He found teacher helpfulness so effective that he called it "the teacher's hidden asset." Nothing else, he said, influences students in such a positive way. He said that, to be most effective, teachers should continually ask themselves the question, "What can I do right now that will be most helpful to my students?"

But Helpful Discipline doesn't rest solely on an attitude of helpfulness. It employs a number of specific tactics, such as meeting students' needs, collaborating with students, making class agreements about behavior and other matters, strengthening class character, and strengthening communication and human relations. These components, what they entail, and how they are put into effect are explained in Chapter 2.

What Is to Come

In the chapters that follow, you will find Helpful Discipline described in detail, together with suggestions for incorporating it into your teaching style. You will find the ideas easy to understand and the procedures easy to implement. As you move forward, you will see how to avoid the major pitfalls normally encountered in discipline: students and teachers at odds with each other, students' avoiding situations they find unpleasant, teachers trying to make students behave, students resisting teacher requests, and the entire process leaving teachers and students nervous, frustrated, and distrustful of each other.

Immediately you will see that Helpful Discipline is not something that stands apart from teaching, but is, instead, an integral part of it. Teaching, discipline, and other aspects of class life are interwoven and must be enhanced together to produce the results we desire. In Chapter 2, you will begin exploring what you can do to provide your students and yourself with this better, more satisfying, and more enjoyable school experience.

QUESTIONS FOR SELF-IMPROVEMENT

1. Have you seen specific evidence that student behavior is becoming more disrespectful and more dangerous? If so, how does that realization affect you? What do you think you might be able to do about it, if anything?

2. It was said that all teachers want their students to learn well and behave themselves appropriately. Why do you think teachers have had difficulty reaching those goals?

3. It was claimed that Helpful Discipline can improve student behavior when more forceful approaches have not. Do you, at this point, consider this claim realistic?

ACTIVITIES FOR SELF-IMPROVEMENT

1. Name specific student misbehaviors you think teachers find most troubling. What do you think you might be able to do, aside from punishing students, to reduce those behaviors?

2. One element of Helpful Discipline is teachers' modeling appropriate behavior. Name some of the specific behaviors you think teachers should model.

3. Identify some of the potential benefits you see in Helpful Discipline. Identify some of the difficulties or problems you think it might present.

2 Moving toward Helpful Discipline

This chapter further explains Helpful Discipline, its nature, and how it functions. Tasks are identified that one must complete in order to make Helpful Discipline operational in the classroom.

The Traits of Helpful Discipline

In Chapter 1 you read that Helpful Discipline is the most effective discipline approach available to today's teachers. Here are its main characteristics:

- It is always helpful, never forceful.
- It places great emphasis on ethics, trust, and joy in the classroom.
- It is aligned with students' needs and the goals of education, which it always promotes and never contravenes.
- It gives attention to teacher needs, recognizing that teachers cannot contentedly use a discipline approach that disregards their needs.
- It is collaborative. Teacher and students work together to establish and conduct class agreements and procedures.
- It is proactive rather than reactive. It anticipates behavior problems in advance and determines how to prevent or deal with them.
- It emphasizes self-control and helps everyone assume greater responsibility for their own behavior.
- It stresses ethical character and continually strives to strengthen it.
- It promotes quality communication and human relations.

Tasks Involved in Implementing Helpful Discipline

If you wish to implement Helpful Discipline in your classroom, you must carry out twelve tasks, previewed here. The preview shows more fully the nature of Helpful Discipline and the procedures it entails. Each of the tasks receives further attention in chapters that follow.

Task 1. *Examine concepts you hold about discipline. Remove erroneous or counterproductive concepts and replace them with productive ones.* Most of us believe things about discipline that don't correspond fully with what we know about students and their natural behavior. Our concepts of discipline are at times counterproductive to what we hope to achieve. Examples of such nonproductive concepts are:

Discipline is what teachers do to students when they misbehave at school.
Students misbehave because they have bad intentions and poor attitudes.

In Chapter 3, we will see why these and certain other concepts inhibit good discipline, and we will explore more useful concepts that should replace them.

Task 2. *Familiarize yourself with seven fundamental human needs and their associated surface needs and behaviors. Learn how needs influence behavior and can be used to advantage.* The behavior of people of all ages is motivated to a large extent by seven psychological needs: security, belonging, hope, dignity, power, enjoyment, and competence. These basic needs are accompanied by a number of "surface needs and behaviors." By attending to surface needs and behaviors you simultaneously address the associated underlying need.

The seven needs are persistent and seem to change little over the course of our lives. Because they are so powerful, you must organize your program to meet them. By doing so, you free students to learn rapidly and enjoyably. Misbehavior usually occurs when needs are thwarted or left unmet. Student needs are considered in detail in Chapter 4, and teacher needs in Chapter 5.

Task 3. *Identify your own basic needs and make sure your teaching and discipline systems are consistent with them.* Educators have long suggested that teacher needs don't matter much, that they can be disregarded provided the program meets students' needs. This simply is not true. Teachers are never comfortable using tactics that stifle their personal needs. Ultimately, they abandon those tactics in favor of others, even when they are not in students' best interests. To work effectively with students, you must make sure your program meets your needs as well as theirs.

Task 4. *Adjust your curriculum and instruction to maximize their compatibility with human needs and the goals of education.* You have just seen the seven basic needs that are common to all people. By adjusting instruction to satisfy those needs, you automatically reduce misbehavior. You further improve instruction and discipline by clarifying precisely what you are trying to accomplish in your classes regarding learning, attitudes, and character. This clarification helps keep your program on track. Suggestions for making these adjustments are presented in Chapter 6.

Task 5. *Present yourself attractively to your students.* Students want teachers who are enthusiastic, interesting, kind, caring, and helpful. We see these traits in teachers we call "charismatic." Students support such teachers and want to associate with them and please them. There are many things you can do to present yourself in a more interesting light, as explained in Chapter 7.

Task 6. Learn what is meant by teacher–student collaboration, understand how it affects teaching, learning, and discipline, and determine how you will use it in your classes. Close collaboration between you and your students produces two exceptional benefits. First, it puts the two of you on the same side, working together to promote quality education; second, it removes the adversarial relationship so often seen between teachers and students in which each seems to be trying to gain the upper hand. Collaboration is examined in greater detail in Chapter 8.

Task 7. Learn what is meant by misbehavior, recognize the types of misbehavior that normally occur in the classroom, and identify the factors that cause misbehavior. In Helpful Discipline, misbehavior is considered to be any behavior that, through *intent or thoughtlessness*, interferes with teaching or learning, threatens or intimidates others, or oversteps society's standards of moral, ethical, or legal behavior. In Chapter 9 you will find descriptions of the major types of misbehavior along with factors that cause students to misbehave. There you will see that misbehavior is most accurately viewed as behavior that naturally occurs from the interplay between student nature and conditions existing at a given time.

Task 8. Learn to remove, deactivate, or ameliorate the causes of misbehavior that originate in individuals and groups. Causes of misbehavior that you can address reside in four locations: individual students, groups of students, learning environments, and adult educational personnel. It is necessary that you learn how to remove, deactivate, or ameliorate the causes of behavior that reside in individuals and groups of students. By successfully doing so, you prevent or correct corresponding misbehavior.

Task 9. Learn to address causes of misbehavior that originate in instructional environments and school personnel. It is also necessary that you learn to remove, deactivate, or ameliorate causes of behavior that originate in classrooms, gymnasiums, shops, libraries, and the like, as well as in adult educational personnel such as teachers, administrators, librarians, and other adults at school. As you do so you simultaneously reduce the incidence of misbehavior.

Task 10. Learn how to prevent misbehavior, support student self-control, and correct misbehavior in a positive manner. Preventive discipline requires relatively little effort but brings great payoffs. Supportive discipline helps students regain self-control when they are on the verge of misbehaving. Corrective discipline is applied to stop misbehavior, get students back on track, and preserve positive feelings and relations. Tactics useful in prevention, support, and correction are presented and discussed in Chapter 12.

Task 11. Learn what is meant by class character, the effects it has on learning and behavior, and how it can be strengthened. Class character can be thought of as the personality of your class. It is comprised of a number of separate qualities such as ethics, trust, and energy, all of which can be improved. Those qualities and the means for strengthening them are described in Chapter 13.

Task 12. *Learn how communication and human relations can be used to improve the overall quality of your class.* Good communication and good human relations help students get along with you and each other better and more willingly. Both emphasize making good impressions on others, opening up dialog, and conferring dignity. Suggestions for making these skills part of daily life in your classes are presented in Chapter 14.

QUESTIONS FOR SELF-IMPROVEMENT

1. In Chapter 1, the claim was made that the strategies embodied in Helpful Discipline comprise the only truly effective approach to discipline for most of today's classes. From what you have read so far, what do you think is the basis for that statement? To what extent do you think the statement is correct?

2. One of the key components of Helpful Discipline is collaboration between teacher and students. Do you agree with the rationale for such collaboration? Can teachers and students be genuine collaborators when teachers must retain ultimate authority?

3. Having read the tasks that must be completed if you wish to move toward Helpful Discipline, what is your appraisal of the probable benefits from this discipline approach, and what is your reaction to the preliminary effort required?

ACTIVITIES FOR SELF-IMPROVEMENT

1. Review the list of tasks suggested for implementing Helpful Discipline. At this time, which three tasks seem to you most important, and which three least important for effective discipline?

2. Nine statements were made concerning the traits of Helpful Discipline at the beginning of the chapter. In your own words compose a half-page written description of Helpful Discipline based on the nine statements.

3. Analyze your present competencies in the 12 tasks preliminary to installing Helpful Discipline. In which are you strongest? In which are you weakest?

3 Establishing Productive Concepts about Discipline

This chapter explores eight counterproductive concepts educators often hold about discipline that hinder its effective implementation. The errors in those concepts are described and more accurate concepts are suggested in their place. Please check yourself to make sure your concepts of discipline are not hindering the quality of your teaching.

Re: Insoluble Discipline Situation

Inaccurate concept: *The discipline problem is so complex, unwieldy, and ingrained that we can do little besides learn to live with it.* This concept suggests that we are unable to do much about the discipline problem, that it will always be a problem, and that all we can reasonably do is make the best of a shabby situation.

More accurate concept: *Misbehavior is caused by specific, identifiable factors we can do something about.* Students are not preprogrammed to misbehave, although some certainly try to test limits and boundaries. You are on the track to improving behavior once you recognize that misbehavior is produced by causes you can control. Instead of believing that it is your lot to struggle with disrespectful, unmotivated students, please understand that you have the power to make behavior and class life better for your students and yourself.

Re: Student Desire to Behave Properly

Inaccurate concept: *With few exceptions, all students can behave properly if they want to. Thus, when they misbehave it is because they willfully decide to do so.*

This statement is enigmatic. It is largely true, yet, at the same time, when accepted uncritically it can encourage you to believe that today's students prefer to behave improperly and make your life miserable.

More accurate concept: *Students are not preprogrammed to misbehave. For the most part, their natural behavior in specific situations is simply incompatible with our expectations.*

It is true that students can choose *not* to misbehave, at least when given time to think, but much of their disruptive behavior occurs reactively within the situations where they find themselves, as when others provoke them or they are bored out of their wits. Instead of telling ourselves that students can behave well if they want to, and that it's their fault when they don't, we should concentrate on this question: "What can I do to help my students behave properly in a natural manner or because they see the advantage of doing so?" Much of this book is directed at answering those questions.

Re: Student Intentions and Attitudes

Inaccurate concept: *Students misbehave because they are ill-intentioned and have bad attitudes.*

Students do, at times, try to subvert teacher efforts or intimidate or harm others, but it is erroneous and counterproductive to conclude that all misbehavior stems from bad attitude and evil intention. Is spontaneous Marcia really ill-intentioned when she forgets herself and excitedly talks during designated quiet time? Is dreamy Alex really in the clutches of evil when he looks out the window and wonders what it would feel like to fly through those clouds?

More accurate concept: *Misbehavior usually occurs naturally from the interplay between student nature and conditions existent at a particular time.* Students frequently misbehave when they are threatened, provoked, or insulted. These reactions occur naturally, not from students plotting mischief. Our job is to eliminate insofar as possible the class conditions that promote or allow misbehavior to occur. We know how to do this, as will be shown later.

Re: Assigning Blame for Misbehavior

Inaccurate concept: *Misbehavior is the fault of students, or of parents, or of teachers, or of society.*

This statement contains much truth, yet finding fault and placing blame do nothing to improve discipline. In fact, blaming usually has the opposite effect: It offends whoever gets blamed and deflects attention from the causes of misbehavior we can do something about. Blaming can only make situations worse.

More accurate concept: Misbehavior occurs for specific reasons. We can identify those reasons and eliminate them or ameliorate their effects.

Admittedly, we can do little about conditions in society that cause students to misbehave. However, we know of at least twenty causes of classroom misbehavior that we can eliminate or ameliorate. As we attend to those causes, student misbehavior decreases correspondingly.

Re: When Discipline Is Applied

Inaccurate concept: *Discipline is what teachers do to stifle misbehavior when it occurs.*

This concept suggests that discipline does not come into play until after students misbehave. That after-the-fact approach is called "reactive discipline." It is central to what we call old-fashioned discipline whereby teachers, when students misbehave, take action to stop the misbehavior, such as calling students by name, admonishing them, or invoking stringent consequences. This reactive tactic has notable limitations and is relatively ineffective in helping students conduct themselves responsibly.

More accurate concept: *Good discipline is a broad strategy we carefully plan in advance to help students, and ourselves, profit best from the school experience.* It entails far more than simply reacting to misbehavior. It Instead of waiting for students to misbehave and then taking steps to "correct" their actions, we anticipate, plan for, and prevent difficulties that normally arise in the classroom. We attend to what is likely to please students and what might cause them to react adversely, and we use communication and human relations to advantage. We do not do these things unilaterally, but in collaboration with our students, insofar as possible. This approach involving anticipation and preplanning is called "proactive discipline."

Re: Effective Discipline Involves Force and Coercion

Inaccurate concept: *In order to be effective, discipline must rely on elements of fear backed by force.*

This has always been the traditional view of discipline, that students will not behave themselves unless fearful of the consequences. For that reason, threat, fear, coercion, and force have been staples of discipline.

More accurate concept: *Force, coercion, and threat are detrimental to effective discipline and should be replaced with consideration, kindness, and helpfulness.* We now know that threat and force produce undesirable resistance, fearfulness, hesitancy, dislike for teacher and school, and thoughts of gaining revenge.

Discipline cannot be called effective unless it preserves positive feelings and good will. Scolding and reprimanding should be replaced with consideration, helpfulness, and other tactics that encourage students to behave desirably. We want students to behave acceptably because they feel like doing so, not because they are afraid of what we will do to them.

Re: Teacher Relationships with Students

Inaccurate concept: *Teachers automatically know how to relate productively with students.*

As a matter of fact, teachers do often have a natural talent for relating well with students and are good at human relations in general. Yet most of us can learn to relate more effectively than we might imagine. All of us have good intentions toward students, but many of us, because of habit, frustration, affronts received, or simple lack of knowledge, sometimes do things that provoke conflict, inhibit learning, and leave the class dispirited.

More accurate concept: *We can improve the ways we relate to and work with students.* The key is to move into a collaborative mode in which we work with students from a position of social equality. This takes us out of the "boss" mentality in which we direct students as if they were social inferiors expected to comply with our wishes.

Fortunately, we know many relational tactics that help students feel safe, respected, empowered, and appreciated. Your effectiveness increases as you use them instead of making students feel hurt, resistant, or vengeful. This reassures students you have their interests at heart and will do all you can to help them succeed. They, in turn, become more willing to follow your lead and cooperate with you.

Re: Tampering with the Curriculum

Inaccurate concept: *The curriculum as presented in curriculum guides and textbooks shouldn't be tampered with.*

Curriculum has a great deal to do with discipline, as you will see in Chapter 6. Many teachers feel that, because the curriculum has been expertly prepared to suit students at different stages of development, it should be covered in its totality without change. Frequently, however, students find certain curriculum topics boring and meaningless, which can lead to misbehavior.

More accurate concept: *Modify the curriculum as necessary to make it interesting, meaningful, and pleasurable for your students.* Instead of thinking that the curriculum is sacrosanct, even when you can see it is out of sync with students' needs and interests, understand that you can and should make adjustments as needed. Students resist subjects they find too hard or too boring or meaningless, and if you try to "make" them learn anyhow you can expect them to resist and otherwise misbehave. You are usually allowed to make reasonable changes in the curriculum if they help students learn better, enjoy the process, and maintain desirable attitudes.

QUESTIONS FOR SELF-IMPROVEMENT

1. Which two of the eight somewhat inaccurate concepts do you suspect teachers most often harbor? Which two do you think are least common?

2. In relation to the concept of tampering with the curriculum, what precautions would you take to deflect criticism that might come your way from parents or administrators who learn you are changing the standard curriculum?

3. Suppose you know achievement tests contain items that are taught in portions of the curriculum your students find deadly boring. What do you do in that case?

ACTIVITIES FOR SELF-IMPROVEMENT

1. Test yourself on the eight somewhat erroneous concepts presented in this chapter. Which two have most characterized your thinking about discipline? Which two have least characterized it?

2. Examine the following "blaming" statements and see if you can replace them with helpful statements:

   a. Bobby is very aggressive on the playground. What can you expect? His whole family is that way.

   b. Carlos is bright enough, he just doesn't want to try. He would rather sit and day-dream.

   c. It's no wonder that Jarron lies and steals, growing up in that neighborhood.

   d. Aaron was born angry and hostile. Nothing is going to change him.

PART TWO

Attending to Needs of Students and Teachers

Part 2 explores more deeply the basic human needs that affect behavior in school. You will learn how to identify those needs and understand how they affect behavior. You will see that, when basic needs go unmet, associated needs and behaviors come to the surface, and that, by attending to those surface manifestations, you simultaneously satisfy the underlying basic need. Finally, you will examine ideas for improving the quality of your program by aligning it with human needs and the established goals of education.

CHAPTER

4 Student Needs that Affect Behavior

In this chapter we examine seven basic human needs that strongly affect class behavior. Unmet needs lead to misbehavior and discipline, to be effective, must help students meet their needs while never working against them. "Surface behaviors and needs" arise when basic needs are not adequately satisfied. As we help to satisfy them, we simultaneously satisfy the corresponding basic needs.

Basic Human Needs

Humans have a number of basic needs that must be met continually. When any of them is left unsatisfied for long, behavior and attitudes can deteriorate. Seven of those basic needs are especially important in school:

- Security—We want to be safe, free from personal danger.
- Belonging—We want to be acknowledged as a worthwhile person and be a valued partner or member of a group.
- Hope—We want sincerely to believe that things will continue well or get better, that a rosy future lies ahead.
- Dignity—We crave respect from others, and we want to think of ourselves as admirable people.
- Power—We desire a degree of control in our lives, over people, conditions, and events that affect us.
- Enjoyment—We want to have fun and find satisfaction in what we do and those we associate with.
- Competence—We want to be able to do things well and know that others think we are competent.

When these needs are being met satisfactorily, students participate in school contentedly and productively. When any of them is not being met, students feel a moderate to strong sense of discontent. That discontent motivates new behavior, which at times may be positive, as when students redouble their efforts to learn, but more often is negative, as when Julie, new to the school, withdraws into herself and refuses to take part in class activities.

It is up to you to determine why Julie behaves as she does and what you can do about it. Perhaps by talking with Julie you can learn of her feelings of isolation or powerlessness, feelings that often arise when the need for security goes unmet, even for a little while. When you talk with Julie and attend to her needs, you can bring her back into a productive mode.

Surface Behaviors Related to Basic Needs

We can usually tell when students are troubled, but it is not easy to identify which basic need is causing the difficulty. In Julie's case, she behaves by withdrawing and refusing to participate. You may decide that her need for security is not being met and that she is trying to protect herself by withdrawing. Meanwhile, Alex's outbursts are disrupting your class. Do they relate to his need for belonging or to something else? And Maria is very lethargic and unmotivated. Which of her needs is going unmet?

By carefully observing exactly what students do when their behavior is problematic and by chatting with them, you can usually pinpoint the underlying need that requires attention. That is possible because basic needs, when unmet, produce related behaviors that give us clues to the underlying problem. We call those related behaviors "surface behaviors" because they are evident and observable, not hidden beneath the surface. When we attend to those behaviors in a positive manner, we simultaneously satisfy the need responsible for them.

Student Needs and Activities Related to Them

The needs-and-gratification paradigm can be understood as follows: (1) A basic needs goes unmet; (2) surface behaviors arise that indicate that a basic need requires attention; (3) we attend to the surface behaviors in a positive manner that satisfies the underlying need, at least temporarily. The following paragraphs show surface behaviors commonly related to basic needs, along with suggestions for providing the attention they require.

1. *Related to the basic need for security:* Students trying to meet the need for security show surface behaviors that call for closeness to or contact with the teacher, kindness from others, and safety in all places and activities. Some of these behaviors, such as a constant clamoring for attention, may annoy you, while you hardly notice others, such as students' retreating into places, activities, and association with other students that pose little threat. If these surface behaviors do not bring the results students want—or, worse, if they bring disapproval—students may then withdraw further, feign incompetence, or simply refuse to try, as Julie did.

Suggestions: Help students satisfy the need for security by providing a classroom safe from threat and harm. Show them personal attention and kindness. Make it clear to your students that you do not expect them to be perfect, that you know they will make mistakes, and that making mistakes is a valuable way of learning. Discuss the importance of helping everyone feel comfortable, meaning that they are accepted without disapproval for what they are and what they do. As you do these things, reticent students begin to feel comfortable enough to participate in class activities.

2. *Related to the basic need for belonging:* Students trying to meet the need for belonging display surface behaviors that call for personal attention, acknowledgment from teacher and peers, establishing friendships, and being included in groups. Seeking attention is very common, as when Shawon shouts out in class and tries to get others to acknowledge and validate him. When unsuccessful with these behaviors, students may hang about on the fringes of groups and try to curry favor. They may bond with students who are like themselves. They may adopt a "sour grapes" manner, or bully or intimidate those weaker than themselves.

Suggestions: Help students satisfy the need for belonging by making sure they receive personal attention every day, not only from you but from fellow students as well. Establish friendly working relationships in which students participate meaningfully in groups. Give students responsibilities for attending to the well-being of other students and the class environment. These tactics provide helpful personal contact and a sense of importance, thus eliminating most attention-seeking behavior.

Linda Albert (1996) advises teachers to help students meet the need for belonging by enabling them to "connect" with others through positive relationships. As students make these connections, they become more cooperative and helpful with each other and more receptive to teachers. To facilitate making these connections, Albert stresses what she calls "The Five A's": acceptance, attention, appreciation, affirmation, and affection.

Acceptance means understanding that it is all right for each person to be as he or she is, regarding culture, abilities, disabilities, and personal style.

Attention means making oneself available to others by sharing time and energy with them.

Appreciation involves acknowledging the accomplishments of others by giving compliments, expressing gratitude, and describing how other individuals have helped the class.

Affirmation involves making positive statements about others that emphasize desirable traits, such as courage, cheerfulness, dedication, enthusiasm, friendliness, helpfulness, kindness, loyalty, originality, persistence, sensitivity, and thoughtfulness. Affirmations should be phrased as, "I have noticed your thoughtfulness" and "Your kindness is always evident."

Affection refers to displays of kindness and caring that people show each other. It is freely given, with nothing required in return.

---

3. *Related to the basic need for hope:* Students trying to meet the need for hope seek tangible evidence of progress in learning. They want to see their skills improve. They want many opportunities to experience success and they enjoy contemplating a bright future. In attempting to meet these needs, students often boast about their prowess, real or imagined, tell how good things were elsewhere or in the past, and continually ask for approbation and verification of progress and competence. When these surface behaviors do not bring what students are seeking, students tend to become lethargic. They may stop trying. Older students may begin thinking of dropping out of school. Others gravitate to peers who share their feeling of hopelessness.

Suggestions: Help students satisfy their need for hope by encouraging them to learn meaningful skills in areas of personal interest. Help them document what they have learned, and discuss new learnings they will acquire in the future. Show them that every day in the classroom can be enjoyable and worthwhile.

4. *Related to the basic need for dignity:* Students trying to meet the need for dignity seem to desire frequent achievement, success, and recognition. They want to have their personal qualities and accomplishments acknowledged. They react poorly to being teased or called names. For those reasons they often seek acknowledgment from teacher and peers. They tend to be overly sensitive while imagining or wanting to believe themselves superior to others. They are prone to putting others down. If these behaviors don't bring them satisfaction, students may become overly defensive, feel victimized, and react hostilely to perceived slights or disrespect.

Suggestions: Help students satisfy their need for dignity by treating them as competent and valuable members of the class, able to assume important tasks and conduct themselves responsibly. Talk with them personally, as your social equals. If necessary, conduct lessons that show students how to react appropriately when threatened or provoked.

5. *Related to the basic need for power:* Students trying to meet the need for power often display surface behaviors that call for respect and admiration. They want to engage in significant collaboration with others and want to hold responsible positions in groups and the class. They try for special collaboration with the teacher and powerful students and attempt to exert influence in class decisions. When these behaviors are unsuccessful, these students may try to exert control over others who are less powerful. They often become belligerent and vociferous and may engage in power struggles with the teacher.

Suggestions: Help students satisfy their need for power by bringing them into collaborative decision making and putting them in charge of tasks important to the class. This reduces their negative power-seeking behavior.

6. *Related to the basic need for enjoyment:* Students trying to meet the need for enjoyment usually try to associate with others they like, and they desire instructional activities that are fun, challenging, and intriguing. They like cooperative activities with other students and are drawn to charismatic teachers. They frequently seek interesting things to do that are not related to the lesson. (If you are presently teaching, you've had ample experience with this behavior.) When these behaviors do not bring satisfaction, students talk, move about, and act out. They seek things to do other than the assigned activities.

Suggestions: Help students satisfy their need for enjoyment by providing instructional topics and activities they find engaging and, when appropriate, allowing them to work in groups with others, one of their favorite activities in school. Maintain a balanced sense of humor. Let students have a good laugh from time to time. Call attention to the fun and enjoyment that can be found in most matters.

7. *Related to the basic need for competence:* Students trying to meet the need for competence need tangible evidence of growth in prowess and progress in learning. They usually know they heed your help and support. They like to see how school learnings apply to real-life situations. They seek opportunities to excel, and they want praise, congratulations, and laudatory comments from others. When these behaviors do not bring satisfaction, students become frustrated. They exaggerate their achievements. They show off or boast excessively and say uncomplimentary things about teachers, school, and program.

Suggestions: Help students satisfy their need for competence by providing the opportunity and support they need to become excellent in academics, physical skills, special interests, and other matters they consider important. Find ways for them to demonstrate new capabilities to themselves, peers, parents, and others.

QUESTIONS FOR SELF-IMPROVEMENT

1. Imagine what it would be like to live in insecure, dangerous surroundings, cut off from family and friends, with no hope that conditions would ever improve. How, specifically, do you think that would affect your daily behavior?

2. We speak of needs as permanent and always active throughout life. What role if any do you feel needs play in the desire to eat chocolate, view a particular movie, or watch the school basketball game?

3. Your student Jonnie talks back, resists doing what you request, and tries to boss other students. What need, if any, do you think Jonnie is unknowingly trying to satisfy?

4. Kristi raises her hand to answer every question you ask. She answers out in class. She gives explanations even when they are not required. She does many "cute" things such as tossing her head and making faces. What need, if any, do you think Kristi is trying to satisfy?

ACTIVITIES FOR SELF-IMPROVEMENT

1. Review the seven human needs described in this chapter. Which two do you think most influence today's students? Which two do you think have the least influence?

2. Have the seven needs affected you as an adult student? If so, explain how.

3. Think of a student you have known personally who did not react well to school. Could that student's needs have been met so that school became helpful to him or her? Explain.

4. Author Richard Curwin (1992) has said that giving students hope is our greatest teaching asset. Explain in a half page what you think he probably means by that.

5 Teacher Needs and the Attention They Require

This chapter explores teacher needs and explains why they require attention. As in Chapter 4, basic needs are presented and "surface needs" associated with them are identified. As you satisfy your surface needs, you simultaneously satisfy your basic needs, essential if Helpful Discipline is to work effectively.

The Importance of Teacher Needs

It was mentioned earlier that, for discipline and teaching to be fully effective, we teachers must get our needs met in the classroom, too. It is time to stop pretending that we can happily forget about our needs so long as our students are satisfied. This isn't the way human nature works, even among the most dedicated teachers.

We have the same basic needs as students, and we try to meet them much as students do. We want to be *secure* in our classrooms, schools, and jobs. We want to feel that we *belong,* that we are accepted by colleagues, administrators, parents, and students. We always *hope* for a better and brighter future. We want to maintain a genuine sense of *dignity,* of self-respect. We want *power* in selecting, organizing, and presenting a curriculum we think best for our students, and we want to be accepted as one who can adjudicate disputes with, and among, students. We want to have an *enjoyable* time working with students and feel the satisfaction of seeing them grow and improve. And we want to feel ourselves becoming ever more *competent* in our skills of teaching and relating with students.

For our sense of well-being, and for fully competent job performance, we have to meet those needs. Traditional discipline—the coercive type—has never helped us in that regard because it works against all our needs except one, power. When we try to control students forcefully, they do not respond to us as we would like them to. Yet, we continue resorting to force because we don't know how else to control misbehavior. The harder we try to make students behave, the more resistant they become, and the more they resist, the more we turn to heavy-handed tactics. You can see how this circular process causes ever-increasing frustration.

This needn't happen. When students really believe we are trying to help, rather than force, they rally to us, support us, and show appreciation for our efforts. When they cooperate with us, the class accomplishes a great deal. When we enliven our curriculum and teaching, students enjoy school and consider it worthwhile. When we communicate with students effectively, they grow quickly in confidence, motivation, self-direction, and responsibility. When we see these results, we certainly enjoy ourselves and feel competent and successful. That is how we can best meet our needs in school.

Surface Needs of Teacher

If somebody asked us about our needs as teachers, it's not likely we'd mention security, belonging, hope, dignity, power, enjoyment, or competence. Instead, we would mention surface manifestations of those needs, such as being trusted, appreciated, paid more, and freed from senseless duties. By examining our "surface needs" we understand what our psyches require. The following illustrations show teacher surface needs related to underlying needs.

1. *Related to the basic need for security:* We teachers always hope we won't receive threatening behavior from students, administrators, or parents. We long for positive student behavior, kind considerate treatment, support from administrators and fellow teachers, and the admiration of students' parents. Like everyone else, we have a strong need for security. When it is not being met, we become fearful, nervous, erratic, and overly defensive.

Suggestions: You can meet the need for security by making sure you clearly understand your professional obligations and how to meet them. You can establish quality relationships with students, thereby gaining their support. You can reach agreements with them that specify how they will conduct themselves and what should be done to help them when they misbehave. You can establish contact with parents and show you are working hard for their children's benefit. Most parents strongly support you when you show special interest in their child.

2. *Related to the basic need for belonging:* We always seem to experience surface needs for students to acknowledge us, in a kindly manner, as a person central to their well-being, someone they couldn't easily do without. We need to receive from them occasional expressions of gratitude and appreciating. Most of us want camaraderie with professional associates. We like to be thought of as important members of the school. When the need for belonging is not being met, we often become abrasive or even sour to students and colleagues. We may become standoffish and reclusive or, in contrast, overly fawning and solicitous.

Suggestions: You can meet the need for belonging by cultivating friendships with colleagues, which will lead to professional bonds of mutual interest and support. You can (and should) participate actively in faculty meetings and school events, looking for ways to establish that you are a member of a professional group engaged in important activities. Through close cooperation with students, you can form a sense of mutual enterprise, working together to make the educational experience the best it can be.

3. *Related to the basic need for hope:* We teachers seem to feel strong surface needs to see our students learn and develop positive attitudes. We need conditions that allow us to give personal attention to students, and we need support and compliments from parents and administrators. When the basic need for hope is not being met, we often become overly demanding. Ultimately, we may become deflated and embittered. The sad fact is that this embitterment results largely from our own actions.

Suggestions: You can help satisfy your need for hope by documenting students' academic and social progress. You can show parents plans for their children's future learning. You can work with administrators to ensure you have access to needed materials and programs. You can plan continually to improve your educational program. Doing these things will keep you focused optimistically on the future.

4. *Related to the basic need for dignity:* We always seem motivated by surface needs for being treated kindly and respectfully, for student cooperation and congenial compliance, and for acknowledgment of competence and special talents or qualities. How sweet it is when Jason tells others he really likes being in our class, or when Beto happily introduces us to his parents. When our need for dignity is not being met, we often become withdrawn. If this continues for long, we may begin to lose our sense of caring for students and others. A few of us may eventually become overly sarcastic, caustic, and uncaring.

Suggestions: You can meet your need for dignity by holding yourself to the highest standards of professionalism in personal conduct, relations with students and parents, relations with colleagues, and provision of quality education. By continually helping students, you receive commitment from them in return. When you confer dignity on students, parents, colleagues, and administrators, they return it in kind.

5. *Related to the basic need for power:* We always seem to have surface needs for being allowed to organize and present instruction in the professional manner we deem best, to teach without disruption, and to have our suggestions heeded. We want to have input on what is really important in teaching, which in many cases will relieve us of the burden of excessive meetings and paperwork. When our need for power is not being met, we often become frustrated and highly dissatisfied. As time wears on, lethargy replaces frustration. Finally, bitterness predominates.

Suggestions: You can meet your need for power by adjusting curriculum and instruction so they become more suitable for students (you should inform your principal about what you are doing and why). You can consciously take charge of your personal and professional lives and build into them the qualities you find most desirable. You can meet with colleagues and, through gentle persuasion and good example, exert influence that can lead to better education throughout the school.

6. *Related to the basic need for enjoyment:* We always seem motivated by surface needs for positive association with students, parents, and fellow teachers. We desire cooperation from students so we can help them grow academically and behaviorally. We very much want to see students enjoy and appreciate learning. We like to have fun with what we teach and how we teach it. When our need for enjoyment is not being met, we often become dull in spirit. We lose our sense of imagination. Some of us become overly zealous.

Suggestions: You can meet the need for enjoyment, in the short term, by teaching some of your favorite topics using your favorite teaching methods. As you see students having an enjoyable time learning, your pleasure will match theirs. In the long term, you meet the need for enjoyment through the satisfaction of quality relationships with students, colleagues, and parents, as well as through seeing strong improvement in student achievement and behavior.

7. *Related to the basic need for competence:* We always want to feel that, because of our skills, our classes are making good progress. We want to know we are helping students enjoy school and profit from it. We want positive recognition from colleagues. We want to feel growth in our capability to work productively with students. When the need for competence is not being met, we often become overly demanding. If this doesn't give us what we want, we may turn to verbal abuse. When worn out from that, we may withdraw and no longer make much effort.

Suggestions: You can satisfy the need for competence by making sure you remain up-to-date on latest developments in teaching and relating with students. This, combined with successful practice, helps you feel the continual growth you desire. As you see students make good progress under your tutelage, your sense of competence grows. As you show personal interest in each of your students, parents take notice and speak of you as a quality teacher. When you engage in professional development activities, administrators and colleagues begin to acknowledge your competency.

Relation between Discipline and Teacher Needs

If you reexamine teachers' needs, you will see that only one of them can be satisfied through coercive discipline. (You know which one that is.) Intimidating tactics almost always provoke resistance, and continual resistance from students keeps us from meeting all our other needs. We cannot teach contentedly under those conditions.

On the other hand, virtually all our classroom needs will be met if we collaborate closely with our students, remove the causes of misbehavior, and show our students unending concern and helpfulness.

QUESTIONS FOR SELF-IMPROVEMENT

1. Do you feel that students' needs and teachers' needs are approximately the same? If so, why do teachers and students behave differently? Or do they?

2. Often we read admonitions such as "Schools are for students, not teachers," and "The teacher's responsibility is to make education productive for students." These statements seem to suggest that teachers should focus solely on students' needs and never on their own. Do you think teachers should forego their needs for the sake of students? Can both sets of needs be met simultaneously?

3. It might be argued that gratification of needs is not what school should accomplish, that it may be even more important to help students and teachers understand that life does not meet all their needs on a regular basis and that they have to learn to cope with discontent. What is your opinion in that regard?

4. Do the listed surface needs of teachers ring true in your experience? Do your attitudes and behavior suffer when your needs are not adequately met?

ACTIVITIES FOR SELF-IMPROVEMENT

1. Make a persuasive argument for putting teachers' needs and students' needs on an equal footing in discipline.

2. Analyze yourself in terms of your needs for belonging, dignity, enjoyment, and competence. List the surface manifestations of those needs—that is, what you would like to receive or enjoy.

3. Using the seven basic needs, make a list of three things you would assiduously do in the classroom, in relation to each, in order to ensure that your needs are met.

4. Describe how you might explain basic needs to students, indicating what the needs are, how you would try to help students meet their needs, and how you would like for them to help meet yours in return.

Aligning Your Discipline System with Needs and Goals

This chapter explains why your educational program, including your discipline system, should be aligned with student needs, your needs, and the goals of education. Many educators claim that, if your curriculum and teaching are good enough, you won't have to be concerned about discipline. By "good enough," they mean sufficiently interesting that students feel no desire to misbehave. That claim contains a good deal of truth, but how do you produce those conditions in the classroom?

In this chapter you will see how to use needs to energize students, hold their interest, and gain their cooperation. You will also see how your needs come into play and how to align your program with the goals of education.

The Need for Aligning Our Programs

We all know that some classrooms are fun and exciting while others are lethargic and methodical. The difference between the two depends on the quality of subject matter, instructional activities, teacher personality, and system of discipline. In this chapter we examine content and activities. As you improve them, you also improve student behavior. In Chapter 8, you will see how your personality affects students and how you can present yourself attractively, and in Chapters 12 and 13 you will learn how to deal most helpfully with classroom misbehavior.

Where to Begin

One of your most important tasks in teaching is to make the curriculum the satisfying and instruction enjoyable. As you accomplish those tasks, you will find that students learn more, behave better, and have better attitudes. The way to proceed is to make your teaching and discipline programs fully compatible with student needs, your needs, and the goals of education.

Begin with the goals of education. Use them to make sure everything you do in class is aimed at the results expressed in those goals. Anything in your program that does not clearly relate to the desired goals has questionable value. The goals of education explain what we are trying to achieve in education—the knowledge, skills, and attitudes we want students to acquire. Most authorities agree on the following goals:

- *academic learning* of depth and breadth in areas that help us understand and deal with the world, human nature, society, and ourselves;

- *good citizenship*, meaning understanding the nature of democracy and its requirements and how one participates effectively therein;
- a *positive attitude* toward learning, which helps us remain active learners throughout life;
- the ability to *relate well with others*, which enables us to live productively and harmoniously;
- *positive self-control and self-direction*, which help us take charge of our lives and live responsibly.

Relating Curriculum and Instruction to the Goals of Education

Curriculum is the content, or subject matter, you provide to help students reach the goals of education. It promotes acquisition of knowledge, development of academic skills, and positive attitudes and values. *Instruction* is the guidance and activities you provide to help students learn subject matter and develop the targeted skills, attitudes, values, and relationships. Instruction includes ensuring interest in the topic, providing appropriate materials, initiating and guiding purposeful activities, providing practice to strengthen learning, and evaluating progress.

As you think about the activities you provide for students, try to make sure they lead to the goals of education. For example, suppose you allow your students to do the following. Which goals of education do they seem to promote?

work together in groups
memorize information
analyze and solve problems
discuss last week's school dance
play in the playhouse
enjoy free time, so long as it is quiet

Making Your Curriculum Interesting and Worthwhile

We noted earlier that, as a professional, you are expected to establish the curriculum you believe best for your students. You are normally allowed considerable leeway concerning which aspects of the curriculum you will emphasize, which you will cover quickly or not at all, and what additions you will make, if any.

Needs and curriculum. Students find your program attractive if it meets their needs. Do your best to select topics and activities that meet all seven needs at the same time, or at least do not thwart them. However, two needs are indispensable— enjoyment and competence. Stress them first, then do what you can to help students feel safe, an integral part of the class, optimistic, worthwhile, and able to exert influence. Make sure you do nothing that makes students feel fearful, isolated, incompetent, unimportant, or powerless.

Involving students. Discuss with students the subject matter normally covered in class. Explain what it is supposed to accomplish, why it is considered important, and why certain instructional activities are used to explore it. Encourage students to ask questions. This helps them understand what they are expected to learn, how they are expected to learn it, and the reasons behind what they are doing.

When you ask students which subjects they prefer in school, they usually say they like those that are interesting, fun, and worthwhile. Assure your students that, with their help, you will try to make the class reflect their preferences. Seriously consider dropping from your curriculum any topics you know students find boring. If you must teach uninteresting topics (and we often do) teach them through activities students very much enjoy.

Criteria for selection. As you finalize your curriculum, make sure each topic you include meets at least one of the following criteria (see Glasser, 1998b):

- It promotes knowledge or develops a skill that is important in students' lives.
- It is something students have expressed a strong desire to learn.
- It is something you consider especially useful and can be presented through activities students enjoy.
- It is included on achievement tests and college entrance exams.

Curriculum and needs, in review. Whether you make small or large changes in your curriculum, try your best to do the following:

- Make sure everything you teach leads clearly toward the *goals of education.* Eliminate busywork, time fillers, and other aimless activities.
- Emphasize the *usefulness* of everything you teach. If you can't easily explain a topic's usefulness, seriously question whether it belongs in the curriculum. (Sometimes usefulness lies in understanding phenomena and relationships, understanding human effort, and appreciating beauty, fully as much as in practical applications.)
- Let students learn some things they truly *want to know.* They seldom get that opportunity in school. This can sometimes inconvenience you, but the results are worth it.
- Show students how to *organize their own learning and make judgments about it.* Ask them to identify what they hope to achieve or experience. Help them think through what they need to do. Help them gain access to materials and other resources. Ask them to demonstrate or explain what they have learned.

Making Your Instructional Activities Attractive and Effective

All of us want our students to become caring, happy, responsible, curious, creative, and self-disciplined. It is unlikely we can help them develop those qualities if we use instructional activities that are boring and useless. Alfie Kohn says the difference between our intentions and what we ask students to do is particularly unsettling because

> it exposes a yawning chasm between what we want and what we are doing, between how we would like students to turn out and how our classrooms and schools actually work. We want children to continue reading and thinking after school has ended, yet we focus their attention on grades, which have been shown to reduce interest in learning. We want them to be critical thinkers, yet we feed them predigested facts and discrete skills—partly because of pressure from various constituencies to pump up standardized test scores. We act as though our goal is short-term retention of right answers rather than genuine understanding (1996, p. 61).

How, then, can you provide instructional activities that are interesting, yet accomplish what you intend? You do so by attending to students' interests and by involving them in class decisions. Needs and interests tell you what attracts students and what turns them off. By bringing students into the planning process, you increase the likelihood that class activities will be enjoyable.

Teaching style.   William Glasser (1998b) has written a good deal about "boss teachers" and "lead teachers." In the past, most teachers used the boss style, in which they planned everything without involving students, selected the curriculum, and organized instructional activities. While boss teaching organizes and presents information compactly, it does little to invigorate students. The authoritarian nature of boss teaching is off-putting to many students, and it no longer frightens them into behaving properly and doing quality work.

For those reasons, boss teaching is losing favor and is being replaced by lead teaching. Lead teachers try to invigorate students. They ask for student input in selecting appealing instructional topics and activities. They suggest possibilities for how students might do their work and help them secure useful materials. In the process, they continually check students' reactions to activities and progress.

This process motivates students. Nowhere are students much inclined to sit still, keep quiet, work by themselves, write lovely themes, memorize quantities of information, and eagerly knock the socks off achievement tests. They don't like to sit still. They don't like to keep quiet. They don't like to work by themselves and memorize facts. They don't like long reading or writing assignments. They don't like to take tests.

However, students rarely resist if you allow them to talk, work in groups, move about, do creative activities, and collaborate on projects. They enjoy quiet time, too, provided they can do something they enjoy. They very much appreciate variety, novelty, challenge, and mystery. They enjoy team competition and trying to set new standards of personal and class achievement. They like to use computers and media. They like to hear and learn language that has rhythm, rhyme, and metaphor. They like to tell and listen to stories. They like to role-play, perform skits, and give performances. They like rhythmic activities with repetition, music, chanting, clapping, and dancing.

Astute primary teachers often have students clap, hop, and chant when learning, and tell stories that include new reading and spelling words. Secondary teachers have students act out the functions of parts of speech, let them reenact the duties of government officials, and take field trips to local businesses where people describe their duties. School does not need to be dull and never should be. It can be interesting every day. One of your most important challenges is to make it that way, for your benefit as well as your students'.

Remember to Meet Your Needs, Too

In Chapter 5 we noted how important it is that the program meet your needs as well as those of your students, especially your needs for enjoyment and belonging. Curriculum and methods of instruction can be very helpful in this regard. Everyone benefits when you include a topic or two you feel strongly about, know a great deal about, and greatly enjoy discussing, especially when it is something that interests students, too. Of course these topics must be within the parameters of the normal curriculum for your grade or subject. It would be a bit of a stretch (though it could be done) to weave your passion for ornithology into your first-year algebra class, yet it is surprising how many special topics can be related to most areas of the curriculum.

Beyond that, try to teach some of your lessons using activities and materials that appeal to you. If you like to tell stories, do artwork, put on skits, use music, hold debates, or even have students wear special costumes, no need to hold back. You can be sure that the more fun you have while teaching, the more students are likely to appreciate your work, and show it.

QUESTIONS FOR SELF-IMPROVEMENT

1. Which subjects in the school curriculum have you found most interesting? Which least interesting? What have you especially liked or disliked about them?

2. You are receiving the information from this book by reading, which is not a preferred activity for many people. Suppose you were teaching this information to others. How could you increase their enjoyment?

3. Identify one of the best teachers you ever had. How did the person teach, and treat you and the class, that earned your admiration?

ACTIVITIES FOR SELF-IMPROVEMENT

1. Select a subject or topic regularly taught in school that you consider dull and unappealing. Using what students are known to enjoy, indicate what you would do to make the topic not just acceptable, but fun for the students and yourself.

2. Select a subject or grade level. In no more than one page, jot down ideas on how you would provide the best educational program your students ever had.

3. Analyze a real lesson or unit of instruction in terms of how well it leads to the goals of education, meets students' needs, and meets the teacher's needs.

PART THREE

Building Teacher–Student Working Relationships

Part 3 shows how to establish productive working relationships with your students. Emphasis is placed on presenting yourself engagingly to students by using charisma, kindness, helpfulness, and other factors. You will see the importance of involving students in a collaborative partnership in which they work with you in managing the class and resolving difficulties.

CHAPTER

7 Presenting Yourself Engagingly

In this chapter we explore how you can present yourself to students in an appealing manner. Students react strongly to the impressions you make as a teacher and person. Depending on your demeanor, their reactions can be accepting and cooperative or reticent and rejecting. You make the strongest positive impression when you behave in ways that are ethical, helpful, considerate, and charismatic. Students do not misbehave very much when working with teachers they like, admire, and respect.

Showing Your Ethical Self

If you want students to trust you and collaborate as your partners, you must show convincingly that you are honest and fair and will never intentionally harm them or anyone else. To convey this ethical image you must be clear and reasonable about class program, expectations, and working relationships. You must guard against speaking to anyone in a hurtful manner, even when sorely vexed. You must make sure you don't speak disdainfully of colleagues or members of the community. Two marks of your professionalism are courtesy and consideration toward others, even when they show disrespect for you, and pride in your ability to refrain from retaliating when affronted.

This does not mean you should become a floor mat for students. Part of being honest is telling what you stand for and how you feel, especially when students are inconsiderate to you. You must not allow students to run over you, but, at the same time, you must treat them considerately and helpfully.

Showing Your Helpful Self

Students almost always react positively when they see that you are trying to help them. Being helpful does not entail lowering standards or doing students' work for them, nor does it involve trying to "make" students see, understand, work, or behave properly. Rather, it involves meeting students' needs, showing support, asking questions that open new possibilities, and giving hints that help students over hurdles. It involves providing a quality work environment and kind, considerate treatment. It involves showing you want to make the class comfortable and interesting. Through all class routines, and especially in times of turmoil, continually ask yourself, "Is what I am doing right now helpful to my students?" Don't be reluctant to tell students of your desire to help them succeed.

Showing Your Considerate Self

Consideration involves understanding and tactfulness. Considerate teachers try to be aware of students' characteristics, needs, feelings, and circumstances at all times. They understand that any of these factors can affect mood, behavior, participation, and productivity. When you interact with students, be careful how you express opinions, give directions, and provide feedback. Be honest and helpful without giving offense.

Showing Your Charismatic Self

Most of the finest teachers are blessed with charisma that draws students to them. You have probably known several teachers with this attractive quality, which made you want to listen to them, associate with them, and follow their lead.

Some teachers seem singularly lacking in charisma, but could easily improve the impression they make. All of us can do so, genuinely, with no illusions or deceit. You only need to let your outer personality shine. You do this by talking with students in an engaging way, sharing your special talents, knowledge, and skills, and giving them glimpses of your personal life. When you do this, students show interest in you and eagerness to cooperate.

Revealing Your Outer Personality

Personality is the sum total of our individual thoughts, feelings, and behaviors. Depending on how we act, we are said to have a bubbly personality or perhaps one that is vigorous, cynical, moody, or bland. We can artificially separate our personality into two parts: an outer personality we let others see and an inner personality we keep mostly to ourselves.

The outer personality is where you display your charisma. Charisma is personal attractiveness you convey through deep knowledge, facial expressions, friendliness, enthusiasm, bodily carriage, sense of humor, wit, compassion, sensitivity to others, and manner of speaking. Think of those mannerisms for a moment. You might wish to appraise yourself with regard to these characteristics.

Smiles.   Students are attracted to teachers who smile and appear sure of themselves. If smiling doesn't come naturally for you, try practicing. Look your students in the face and give them a group smile and many individual personal smiles. And make them genuine. There is an old Chinese proverb that says, "A man without a smiling face must not open a shop." This applies to teachers as much as shopkeepers.

Friendliness.   Students respond to personal friendliness. You show this quality when you quickly learn and use their names and chat with them individually. You may not be able to speak with each student every day, but at least give them individual greetings, with eye contact and a smile that shows you are pleased they are in the class.

Deep knowledge.   Students enjoy teachers who have breadth of knowledge and deep understanding. They very much enjoy knowing about marvelous or mysterious things and they want to understand natural phenomena. They like discussions in which you analyze past events and speculate knowingly about the future.

Enthusiasm.   Students gravitate to teachers who are enthusiastic, but shy away from those who are not. Enthusiasm, when genuine, enlivens everyone. Not all teachers are naturally enthusiastic. If you are one of those without much pep, practice being enthusiastic until you project it convincingly. Even when your inner personality is down in the dumps, you can keep your outer personality lively.

Sensitivity and compassion.   Students appreciate sensitive teachers who pick up on how they feel and show understanding when they are depressed, disappointed, or hurt. Such teachers don't pretend nothing is wrong, or tell students to buck up, or plow ahead no matter what. Students don't expect you to solve their problems, but they want your sympathy and acceptance. When you see students who seem especially troubled, ask them privately if something is bothering them and if they'd like to talk about it. If they want to talk, arrange a time and place. If they decline, don't pry. Tell them in a warm way you are available to listen if they feel like talking.

Providing Insights into Your Personal Life

Your students definitely want to know about your personal life. Let them in on it, but only in small doses, just an interesting snippet here and there. Students of all ages want to know if you have a spouse, significant other, children, or pets. They like to see photos of them and know what you do on outings. They are eager to know about your hobbies and favorite foods and movies and television programs. These things help students see you as a real person.

You might also share some of your unusual experiences. All of us have done things others find fascinating. We have held unusual jobs, traveled domestically and abroad, or worked in places such as national parks, inner cities, or farms. If you have memorabilia, share some of it with your students occasionally.

Talking Effectively with Students

Talk with students in ways that allow them to drop their defenses and open up to you. When you call them by name and smile and ask how they are, they respond, usually by returning your smile. When you chat with them, they can teach you a great deal if you listen carefully. Never be condescending toward them. Show your interest in them by giving genuine attention. Remember what they tell you about themselves and their interests and mention them later. Encourage them to talk. They like that. It makes them feel important and appreciated.

Sharing Special Knowledge and Skills

All of us have special knowledge and skills that can earn students' admiration. Perhaps you speak a second language and can teach phrases to your students. Perhaps you have worked in a zoo and know details of animals' lives. Perhaps you are an amateur photographer and can show students how to take good pictures. Perhaps you are artistic and can draw caricatures of students. Perhaps you play a musical instrument or sing. Almost all teachers have talents and interests that fascinate students. Share some of yours. They make an attractive impression.

Clarifying Your Leadership Style

We have said a good deal about helping students, about meeting their needs, making them comfortable, making school interesting, bringing them into collaborative partnership, and removing obstacles to acceptable behavior. Because all these efforts focus so strongly on students, you might be getting the impression that teachers function only as helpers while leaving the important decisions to students.

Of course this is not the case. Good learning and good behavior depend on your leadership. It is true that classes function better when students help make decisions and take on important responsibilities, but it is your leadership that makes those things possible. You lead not only in the larger concerns of collaboration, class character, curriculum, instruction, and discipline, but in myriad smaller concerns such as motivation, personal interactions, responsibility, and problem resolution.

A leader is one who raises issues, establishes direction and agenda, sets the tone, makes it easy for others to do their work, provides means for making improvements, and assumes ultimate responsibility. This is what all good leaders do, whether of nations, corporations, or classrooms. They consult with, secure the collaboration of, and delegate responsibility to those over whom they have jurisdiction. This kind of leadership works very well in the classroom.

Different styles of leadership affect students quite differently. We have already seen that, whereas teachers once used a stern authoritarian style, they are progressively moving toward a more democratic style in which they function as guides and mentors, rather than bosses and directors. Students who experience lead teaching tend to work enthusiastically and productively and maintain positive attitudes. Those subjected to boss teaching sometimes work well, too, provided the activities are highly interesting. Oftentimes, however, they find the assigned work tedious, and many do only enough to get by, finding nothing especially appealing about school or teachers.

QUESTIONS FOR SELF-IMPROVEMENT

1. Many people think teacher charisma is overrated. They maintain that teachers needn't rely on charm, but, instead, should organize their programs so students learn easily and remember what they've learned. What is your opinion?

2. Lead teaching was said to produce better results than boss teaching. Is this always the case? What exceptions can you think of?

3. Which aspects of your personal life might you reveal to enhance your charisma? What dangers do you see in revealing too much?

ACTIVITIES FOR SELF-IMPROVEMENT

1. Think of the worst teacher you ever had. Specify what made that teacher bad. Suppose you were asked to help that teacher be more effective. What changes would you suggest?

2. Recall the most charismatic teacher you ever had. Explain what that teacher did that you found so attractive.

3. Analyze your charismatic self in terms of the qualities described. How do you rate on each of them? Where might you improve? Can you make changes in yourself and remain authentic?

8 Working Collaboratively with Students

This chapter explains the advantages of working in close collaboration with your students, describes ways of doing so, and notes the role that collaboration plays in discipline.

The Value of Collaboration

Collaboration refers to working together in close partnership with your students when, together, you plan and make decisions that affect the class. Recent research indicates that students prefer collaborative discipline over any other approach and consider it the most effective (Chiu and Tully 1997; Tully and Chiu 1998).

We have previously noted that collaboration brings a number of desirable qualities to the class. It puts you and your students on the same side so that you can work together to ensure effective teaching, learning, and class behavior. It gives students a much-needed sense of positive power and makes them much more inclined to support decisions they help make. It establishes students' stake in maintaining the well-being of the class and does away with the somewhat antagonistic posture between teacher and students that is seen in most classes. Finally, collaboration makes possible some of the most important aspects of Helpful Discipline, such as such as meeting needs, providing mutual support, developing self-direction and self-control, establishing trust and consideration for others, and building a class sense of community.

The Rationale for Collaboration

The more closely you collaborate with students, the more purposeful and responsible they become. Without collaboration, you are likely to find yourself frequently at odds with them, with neither of you fully able to meet your needs or enjoy the class. With collaboration, the two of you are able to pull together, which increases mutual sensitivity and concern, promotes humane relations, and makes the school experience more satisfactory. We do need to be clear about one thing: Collaboration does not suggest that you and your students always have an equal say in matters that affect the class, nor does it imply that you turn over control to your students. As class leader, you have the final say, and at times may have to veto students' suggestions. In those cases you are obliged to clearly explain your reasons for doing so.

Inviting Students to Collaborate

Students are not automatically predisposed to collaborate with you, and, truthfully, you may not be enthusiastic about having some of them as partners. But if you want to enjoy high quality program and discipline, collaboration is indispensable and it is up to you to bring it about.

You accomplish this through an inductive process of asking students how they like to be taught and treated. Assure them that you want the class to reflect their preferences, but their help is necessary. Ask them if they would be willing to work closely with you to make school more to their liking. Point out that the process requires joint planning and agreements that will guide teaching, behavior, and other class matters.

If, at this point, you wish to see the process fully elaborated, including specific questions you can use, please see "Purposes and Procedures of the Introductory Sessions" in Chapter 15.

Enhancing Collaboration

Once you get the collaborative process in place, there are things you can do to make it work better.

1. *Help students develop a sense of belonging in the class.* Collaboration cannot occur well unless students truly feel they belong in the class, meaning that they perceive themselves as members who are important, worthwhile, and valued. When students receive positive personal attention, they feel valued. When attention is drawn to their accomplishments, they feel important. When they are accepted regardless of their traits or backgrounds, they feel worthwhile. All class members can and should participate in providing a sense of belonging for everyone.

2. *Help the class develop a sense of community.* (Please refer to "Establishing a Sense of Community" later in this chapter.)

3. *Help students gain the confidence they can succeed and contribute.* To raise students' confidence, make it clear that learning is a process of improvement, not an end product. Improvement should be acknowledged as it occurs. Because new tasks seem difficult to everyone, there is little point in calling a task easy or telling students anybody can do it. It is better to tell students, "I know this may seem difficult at first, but keep at it. Let's see how you do."

4. *Involve students meaningfully in decision making.* Treat students as equal, or near-equal, partners in making decisions about various aspects of class life and procedure. They are seldom reluctant to do so in matters that affect their needs. Because schooling often fails to meets students' needs adequately, many make little effort to learn. One of the best things we can do for them is give them a voice in making school interesting and relevant.

5. *Remove students' fear of making mistakes.* The fear of making mistakes undermines students' sense of personal capability. You can minimize this fear through discussions about what mistakes are, the fact that everyone makes them, that they are a natural part of learning, and that the more a person tries to accomplish, the more mistakes he or she will make. Ask students how they feel when others laugh at their mistakes or make fun of them. You might suggest that the class make an agreement that members of the class will not make fun of others' mistakes.

6. *Make sure students see that collaboration is working and they are making progress.* Carefully monitor the collaborative process. Encourage students to express their views about it. Help them recognize their personal progress as they gain knowledge and skills and improve their personal behavior. Grades such as A, B, C do not provide the best evidence of progress. It is preferable that students keep work portfolios that demonstrate their accomplishments and engage in discussions about what they could do in the past, what they can do now, and what they can reasonably expect to do in the future. Students' sense of capability increases when they receive attention for what they've accomplished. This recognition can be given during class and at events such as awards assemblies, class exhibits, and presentations before parents and the public.

Using Collaboration for Positive Power and Self-Direction

Effective collaboration helps students acquire a sense of positive power over their lives and the ability to direct their own behavior responsibly. Students don't learn these skills by talking about them or by your telling them what to do. They need opportunities to make decisions, act on those decisions, and take responsibility for the results. In doing so, they learn from success and mistakes, both of which are powerful teachers. Over time, this process builds an inner sense of discipline, which enables students to deal more effectively with problems they encounter in and out of school.

Because students often make poor decisions when allowed greater decision-making opportunities, you must provide a safe environment in which they can deal with undesirable consequences of their decisions. We need to show respect for students' decisions, even when we are certain they will be unsuccessful. Students learn a great deal from unpleasant consequences of their decisions. One of those learnings is the understanding that they have control over their lives through the decisions they make.

It takes a while for students to develop self-direction and inner discipline. You must be patient while they do so. With each decision-making experience, their ability to resolve problems increases. Don't worry about damage to their self-esteem. It will remain solid because they know they have power, responsibility, and support, and they come to realize that making mistakes is part of the learning process.

As students work through thorny problems on their own, you must resist the temptation to provide solutions for them. You don't want to send the message that students don't have power or capability, or that some other person must take care of them. When students make mistakes, as they will, they don't benefit from being lectured. What they need is an opportunity to correct the situation. The most appropriate thing you can say to them is, "You have a problem. What is your plan for dealing with it?" When students are given ownership of problems and situations, they know it is up to them to make things better.

Barbara Coloroso (1994) says that teachers who wish to help their students develop inner discipline must answer three questions for themselves:

1. What is my goal in teaching?
2. What is my philosophy of teaching?
3. Do I want to empower students to take care of themselves, or do I want to make them wait for teachers and other adults to tell them what to do and think?

Helping Students Share the Load

One of your main goals in collaboration is to help students take on responsibility, not just for themselves but for the class as a whole. Kyle, Kagan, and Scott (2001) refer to this as the principle of shared responsibility, whereby teachers and students share the load, help each other, make joint decisions, take joint responsibility for the results, and help meet each other's needs.

In order to share responsibility equitably, everyone in the class must learn to see situations and problems from the perspectives of others. This means that we must see situations as others see them, even though we may not agree with their views. Such perspective-taking enables class members to recognize others' unmet needs, frustrations, excitement, and satisfaction.

Establishing a Sense of Community

Many authorities now emphasize establishing what they call a "sense of community" in the classroom, in which each person is concerned about the others and all work together for their mutual benefit. Alfie Kohn (1996) is one of the foremost proponents of class community. He says that a sense of community develops as we show caring, provide support, take students seriously, make them feel safe, and bring them into genuine partnership. This allows students to express opinions, make judgments, assume responsibility, and work closely with teachers in seeking solutions to class problems.

And how do you bring about this sense of community? You begin by discussing class matters with students, considering their opinions seriously, and acting on them whenever possible. Students are quite able to understand, given language suited to their development, concepts of needs, helpfulness, consideration, problems, and working together. They know the difference between proper and improper behavior, can see that misbehavior has a number of causes, and can understand how those causes can be removed. They know when they are enjoying learning and when they are not, and can tell you why. They know when they feel treated well, and when they feel slighted or demeaned. They know school suits them better when learning activities are fun and students and teacher treat each other well. Even at an early age they can understand the meanings, and often the advantages, of self-discipline, self-direction, and personal responsibility. As these matters are discussed and students are asked to take part in them and support other members of the class, they develop the sense of "we" that characterizes communities.

As a rule of thumb, ask yourself at every turn how you can involve students in planning class matters. Allow them to help resolve class problems. Allow them to assume responsibility. Involve them in discussing curriculum, teaching, class procedures, and class problems. As you do so, you move away from teaching that "does things to" students and replace it with teaching that treats students as colleagues with important contributions to make.

As part of this process, you stop making rules for students and instead ask them to reach agreements that guide the class. When problems arise, you ask them, "What do you think we can do to solve this problem?" You give up the notion that discipline is for making students quiet and compliant, and you begin looking for ways to help your students become self-directed, responsible, caring, and able to think deeply about topics they find relevant and interesting.

Alfie Kohn (1996) provides a number of suggestions concerning discipline in the classroom community:

- Build trusting, caring relationships with your students. It is much easier to resolve problems when good relationships are in place.
- Learn to listen carefully, remain calm, generate suggestions, and imagine the other person's point of view. Help your students learn to do the same.
- When an unpleasant situation occurs, try to diagnose what has happened and why. Gently ask students to speculate about why they hurt someone's feelings or failed again to complete their assignment. Involving students is more likely to lead to a meaningful, lasting solution than is simply making decisions on your own.
- When students do something cruel, try to help them understand that what they did was wrong, and why. This helps deter similar behavior in the future. Then, an examination should be made of ways to make restitution or reparation, such as trying to restore, replace, repair, clean up, or apologize. Making amends is important and should be viewed as an essential part of the process, but, more importantly, students must construct meaning for themselves around concepts of fairness and responsibility.
- Remain flexible and use judgment concerning when you need to talk with a student about a problem. Sometimes it is better to delay the talk for a while.
- Work with students on coming up with authentic solutions to problems. Instead of looking for easy answers that have no lasting benefit, explore various possibilities open-mindedly. Try to identify the motives behind various behaviors.
- When you must use control, do so in a way that minimizes its punitive impact. A student may be disrupting the class, despite repeated requests not to do so. In that case you may have to isolate the student or send him or her from the room. But even then your tone should be warm and regretful and you should express confidence that the two of you will eventually resolve the problem.

QUESTIONS FOR SELF-IMPROVEMENT

1. What do you see as the value of classes functioning as communities rather than as isolated students? Is community a practical concept, or just a good-sounding idea that won't work in real practice?

2. Four of your major teaching responsibilities are planning lessons, arranging activities, evaluating student work, and maintaining a good working environment. Approximately how much student collaboration would you consider ideal in each of the responsibilities? Explain.

3. To what extent do you feel student collaboration can be used in lower primary grades? Would it be different in higher grades? Explain.

4. Although most teachers agree with the basic principles of collaboration, they worry that the process will take too much time and fail to be sufficiently decisive. Do you agree with those concerns? Explain.

ACTIVITIES FOR SELF-IMPROVEMENT

1. In a half page, express your understanding of collaboration and how it affects class discipline.

2. Suppose student Teresa has been spreading malicious gossip about Marcia, another girl in the class. From a collaborative viewpoint, how do you think you and/or the class could best address the situation?

3. Do you feel student collaboration is as valuable as this chapter seems to indicate? See if you can make a case in favor of strong collaboration and a case against strong collaboration.

4. You might find that some students in your class are eager to collaborate with you while others are reticent. Explain what you would be inclined to do in that event.

PART FOUR

Dealing with Misbehavior and Its Causes

At this juncture we turn attention more directly to misbehavior, to its nature, what causes it, how to deal with the causes, and how to intervene helpfully when students misbehave. We see how misbehavior is defined, note the common types of misbehavior, and explore the known causes of misbehavior. We see how to deactivate or otherwise soften the causes of misbehavior and learn how to deal positively with misbehavior, through prevention, support, and correction.

CHAPTER

9 Understanding the Types and Causes of Misbehavior

This chapter clarifies the meanings of behavior and misbehavior. It identifies thirteen types of classroom misbehavior and twenty addressable factors that cause it.

Meaning of Classroom Misbehavior

Most people think of misbehavior as kids doing what they know they shouldn't. Some feel that certain behaviors, such as sassing the teacher or other adults, lying, and intimidating others, are always misbehavior, regardless of the circumstances in which they occur. Psychologist Thomas Gordon (1989) says misbehavior is a label teachers and parents apply to any behavior they disapprove of, regardless of what it is or where it occurs.

In Helpful Discipline, classroom misbehavior is defined as any behavior that, through *intent* or *thoughtlessness*

1. interferes with teaching or learning;
2. threatens or intimidates others; or
3. oversteps society's standards of moral, ethical, or legal behavior.

We normally think of misbehavior as pertaining only to students, but teachers sometimes misbehave in the classroom, too, as we shall see.

Why Misbehavior Occurs

Classroom misbehavior, although sometimes malicious, usually occurs naturally from the interplay between student nature and conditions that exist at a given time. Janette doesn't often say to herself, "Hey, I think this is a good opportunity for me to misbehave." When she does misbehave she is usually doing what comes naturally to her at a given time, which in her case is usually talking with others when she isn't supposed to. Yet her talking interferes with teaching and learning and, therefore, requires attention.

Janette and other students usually know how they are expected to behave and they usually comply with those expectations. When they don't comply, it is usually for one or more of several "causes" described in this chapter. You can remove those causes, or at least mitigate them, and immediately reduce misbehavior. At the same time, you can provide conditions that make proper behavior more appealing than misbehavior. This sounds easy enough, but it takes a bit of doing.

We used to think students misbehaved because they were born bad, had somehow developed bad attitudes, or harbored a general dislike for teachers and school. It is common to hear teachers say, "That Thomas is a born troublemaker" or "Desiree just wasn't cut out for school." To control those students, we scolded, reprimanded, lectured, assigned extra work, isolated them, and sent them to detention or the principal's office. Those tactics may have been partially effective at one time, but they aren't anymore. That is evident in the poor state of today's classrooms.

However, we are beginning to acquire a new perspective on discipline, one that allows us to exert positive influence that is effective, relatively pleasant, and easy to use. That perspective is embodied in Helpful Discipline. We now understand that most students do not misbehave merely because they consider it the thing to do, but, rather, because of factors such as egocentrism, threat, provocation, fear, boredom, hopelessness, frustration, or feeling isolated. The school experience often worries students and doesn't meet their needs. Bad intentions play little part in misbehavior.

Correcting the Situation

We can now organize class conditions so they lead to proper behavior in a natural manner. You have already explored the beneficial effects of consideration, helpfulness, and meeting students' needs. You have seen how to adjust your program to make it more interesting for students. You have seen how to present yourself engagingly and draw students into a collaborative partnership with you. As you build those functions into your style of teaching, along with others yet to be described, you make school enjoyable and satisfying, which automatically reduces the amount and seriousness of misbehavior. To improve conditions still further, let's take a closer look at misbehavior and what causes it.

Types of Student Misbehavior

Thirteen types of misbehavior are seen in classes everywhere. Discuss them with your students and ask their opinions about how, together, you can keep these misbehaviors from occurring. This helps students understand that misbehavior works against their interests and gets them into trouble, yet is controllable. They also gain insight into how the problems can be remedied.

The thirteen types of misbehavior are:

1. *Inattention*—daydreaming, doodling, looking out the window, thinking about things irrelevant to the lesson
2. *Apathy*—a general disinclination to participate; not caring, not wanting to try or do well
3. *Needless talk*—students chatting during instructional time about things unrelated to the lesson
4. *Moving about the room*—getting up and moving about without permission, congregating in parts of the room
5. *Annoying others*—provoking, teasing, picking at, calling other students names
6. *Disruption*—shouting out during instruction, talking and laughing inappropriately, causing "accidents"
7. *Lying*—deliberate falsification to avoid accepting responsibility or admitting wrongdoing, or to get others in trouble
8. *Stealing*—taking things that belong to others
9. *Cheating*—making false representations or wrongly taking advantage of others for personal benefit
10. *Sexual harassment*—making others uncomfortable through touching, sex-related language, or sexual innuendo
11. *Aggression and fighting*—showing hostility toward others, threatening them, shoving, pinching, wrestling, hitting
12. *Malicious mischief*—doing damage intentionally to school property or the belongings of others
13. *Defiance of authority*—talking back to the teacher; hostilely refusing to do as the teacher requests

Causes of Student Misbehavior

We know at least 20 specific causes of student misbehavior that we can deactivate or reduce. As noted in Chapter 1, causes of misbehavior originate in five realms: the fabric of society, individual students' psyches, class members and groups, instructional environments, and the adult personnel who work with students. We saw that there is little we can do about causes that originate in society, although we can work around them. The causes that originate in the other four realms are all manageable.

Causes that originate within individual students are:
1. *Expediency*: Students look for the easy way, as do all of us. It is sometimes easier to misbehave than to abide by class expectations.
2. The *urge to transgress*: All of us have an urge to see what we can get away with. Occasionally, we give in to it and do what we know we should not.
3. *Temptation*: Students encounter objects, situations, behaviors, people, or other experiences they find powerfully attractive. They adopt, mimic, acquire, or associate with those factors even when doing so leads to misbehavior.
4. *Inappropriate habits*: Students incorporate inappropriate patterns of behavior, acquired in the home and community, and display them in class.
5. *Poor behavior choices*: Students always attempt to meet needs, pursue strong interests, and explore new circumstances. Sometimes their actions are effective and bring approval. At other times they are ineffective and bring disapproval, and are then called "misbehavior."
6. *Avoidance*: We all try to avoid people or situations that are unpleasant or threatening. Sometimes students refuse to participate in lessons or associate with others because they are fearful or don't want to look stupid.
7. An *egocentric personality*: Some students are self-centered or spoiled. They focus on their own desires while disregarding or trampling on the desires and feelings of others.

Causes that originate in class peers and groups are:
8. *Provocation*: Students are often incited to misbehave by classmates or certain situations. They react improperly to annoyance, lack of attention, insult, threat, and boredom.
9. *Group behavior*: Students often succumb to peer pressure or get caught up in group emotion. At those times, they tend to behave—and misbehave—in ways they would not if by themselves.

Causes that originate in instructional environments are:
10. *Physical discomfort*: Students are made restless by inappropriate temperature, poor lighting, and uncomfortable seating and work spaces.
11. *Tedium*: The instructional activities call on students to pay close attention to matters in which they have little interest.

12. *Meaninglessness*: Students are expected to work at topics they do not comprehend or that seem to have no purpose.
13. *Lack of motivation*: Students do not become interested in what they are to learn and, therefore, make little effort.

Causes that originate in school personnel, including teachers, are:

14. *Poor modeling*: Teachers and other personnel may present poor models of ethical, humane, considerate, or helpful behavior, which students then emulate.
15. *Lack of personal attention*: Teachers give students little personal attention, which makes them feel unimportant in the class, not worth the teacher's effort. This reduces motivation and willingness to comply with expectations.
16. *Disregard for students' feelings*: When teachers teach autocratically, speak sarcastically, order students about, point out their inadequacies, and act as though misbehavior is entirely students' fault, students lose motivation, hesitate to cooperate, and sometimes answer back disrespectfully.
17. *Uninteresting lessons*: Teachers provide lessons that do not interest students. Students show little desire to learn or involve themselves in the activities.
18. *Ineffective guidance and feedback*: Teachers do not make clear what students are to do or how to do it. Students therefore remain inactive. Should they complete the work, they receive little indication of whether they have performed appropriately, what they have done well or poorly, and how much progress they have made.
19. *Poor communication*: Students are spoken to in ways that demean, stifle, or threaten, which reduces their willingness to cooperate.
20. *Coercion, threat, and punishment*: Students feel they are being forced or "made" to do things against their will. They become guarded and look for ways to avoid or subvert the perceived force.

All of these causes can be addressed effectively. In Chapter 10 we will see how to deal with causes that originate in individual students and in the group, and in Chapter 11 we will see how to deal with those that originate in instructional environments and school personnel.

QUESTIONS FOR SELF-IMPROVEMENT

1. How do you explain the difference between "helping" students behave appropriately and "making" them behave appropriately? Do you feel the difference is real or a matter of semantics?

2. If someone asked you what is meant by *misbehavior*, what would you say?

3. What sorts of people and situations did you try to avoid in school? Did your avoidance ever cause you to misbehave or miss out on opportunities?

ACTIVITIES FOR SELF-IMPROVEMENT

1. Without looking back at the list, think of five specific student misbehaviors. Review the list of reasons for student misbehavior. Determine whether each of the misbehaviors you identify might be attributed to one or more of the listed reasons. If not, what other reasons might be added?

2. Fear of failure and fear of looking bad in front of others cause many students to withdraw and refuse to participate. Describe some things you might do in your class to reduce this fear.

3. Identify an occasion when, as a student, you violated class expectations. Explain your motivation for doing so. How did the teacher correct you? How might the teacher have corrected you more helpfully?

CHAPTER 10

Addressing Causes of Misbehavior that Originate in Students

This chapter presents suggestions for dealing with the first nine causes of behavior identified in Chapter 9. These causes originate in individual students and groups of students.

Causes that Originate in Individual Students

We saw in Chapter 9 that seven causes of misbehavior originate in individual students: expediency, the urge to transgress, temptation, inappropriate habits, poor behavior choices, avoidance, and an egocentric personality. These causes are sometimes difficult to deal with, but you can significantly reduce the effects of all of them. Consider these suggestions:

1. *Regarding expediency*: Students, as do you and I, try continually to meet their needs and make their lives easier. They take shortcuts, conveniently forget what they know they are supposed to do, look for ways to get out of work, and intentionally break rules. They do these things because they are easier than behaving appropriately. Expedient behavior isn't much of a problem in classes that are interesting and lively, but you see a lot of it in classes that are dull and boring.

Suggestions: Hold discussions with your students about expediency and its troublesome effects. Ask students to explain why they take the easy way, such as reading book summaries or reviews rather than the assigned book, rushing through a writing assignment, or copying others' ideas. They will say it is because they don't like the work, don't see the point in it, or don't want to spend time on it. Ask them what *would* encourage them to give their best effort in school. Listen to what they say and make use of their suggestions if you can.

2. *Regarding the urge to transgress*: Almost all humans feel occasional urges to transgress rules and regulations. Students feel this urge frequently, especially when they don't find their classes appealing. Most occasionally act on the urge and cheat, take shortcuts, tell lies, call names, and annoy others.

Suggestions: Counter this urge through class discussions and your own exemplary behavior. Here are some possibilities and points to keep in mind:

- Discuss the urge to transgress as a natural phenomenon that all of us experience, but that, when acted on frequently, produces unpleasant consequences.

Relate an example or two from your own experience. Ask students to contribute examples as well.

- Discuss the reasons for rules, including how they help us live together harmoniously, how they equalize opportunity, and how, when broken, often make someone suffer unpleasant consequences. You might wish to discuss traffic laws and the accidents and traffic tickets that often result when they are violated, and then move on to class agreements and the reasons behind them.
- Never allow students to see you transgress rules, expectations, or codes of conduct.
- Discuss the meaning of ethics, ethical conduct, and personal character. (This topic is treated in detail in Chapter 13.) Have students tell what they have seen people do that revealed high ethical character. Ask why ethical people are generally admired.
- When you see students abiding by expectations, even when opportunities to transgress are available, draw attention to their behavior and indicate your admiration.

3. *Regarding temptation*: Students regularly encounter objects, situations, behaviors, people, or other experiences they find powerfully attractive. Examples include music and lyrics, desirable objects, ways of speaking, ways of dressing, ways of conducting oneself, and cheating on tests and assignments. Although some of these things are unacceptable in school, students nevertheless find them so attractive they will occasionally do, adopt, mimic, acquire, or associate with them, even though they are forbidden.

Suggestions: Conduct frank discussions with your students in which, together, you analyze temptation and help students understand why certain objects, styles, and opportunities are so seductive, so difficult to resist. Help students foresee the undesirable consequences of adopting disapproved styles and manners. Help them clarify the lines that separate the approved from the disapproved, and reinforce their resolve to resist factors that work against their best interests.

4. *Regarding inappropriate habits*: Inappropriate habits are ingrained ways of behaving that violate standards and expectations. Jason uses profanity. Maria is discourteous, inconsiderate of others, and likes to call them names. Larry always looks for the easy way, even when it requires unacceptable behavior. Josh is aggressive and combative. Some of these habits are learned in school, but most are acquired in the home or community.

Suggestions: Bring inappropriate habits to students' attentions without pointing the finger at any student. Discuss the harmful effects and, if necessary, directly teach your students acceptable alternatives. Topics you might want to consider include poor manners, name-calling, teasing, verbal putdowns, cheating, lying, and disregard for others. Ask your students how they might rid themselves of these undesirable habits and replace them with desirable ones. Help them see that, by doing so, they can present themselves in a better light and make the class more satisfying for everyone. Consider organizing nonthreatening skits and dialogs to help students practice desirable behavior.

5. *Regarding poor behavior choices*: Students often put little thought into how they can meet their needs. Sometimes their needs-related behavior is considered acceptable, and sometimes not. Often the difference is not clear to students. For example, when attempting to meet the need for belonging, Alicia tries so hard to draw attention that she annoys others and they try to avoid her. Alan, trying to meet his need for power, refuses to do what the teacher requests, thereby distressing the teacher and setting a bad example for others. Alicia and Alan are trying to meet legitimate needs, but do not realize that their behavior choices are doing more harm than good.

Suggestions: To help students such as Alicia and Alan, tell the class about surface needs as they relate to basic needs (discussed in Chapter 4). Use the example given there for what students sometimes do when attempting to meet the need for belonging. Discuss questions such as:

- What are some of the things you have seen students do to get attention or be acknowledged?
- What have you seen them do to try to feel they are members of groups and teams?

As students name behaviors they have noted, ask them:

- Does their behavior usually get them what they want?

Write the behaviors on the board under a "yes" column or a "no" column. For behaviors in the "no" column, ask the class:

- What do you think the student could have done that would have brought better results?

For behaviors in the "yes" column, ask students,

- As time passes, will the person's efforts still be effective, or will they produce undesirable results?

6. *Regarding avoidance*: Oftentimes, students misbehave in trying to avoid people or situations they fear or greatly dislike. We need to help them decide when avoidance is appropriate and how they can deal with unpleasant situations they might encounter. No one likes to face up to failure, intimidation, ridicule, and unpleasant people and events. In those circumstances, avoidance is natural and is often the best way to deal with the issue. But in school we can't always avoid things we find unpleasant. Avoidance becomes misbehavior if it affects teaching or learning, or is unethical, harmful, or disrespectful to others. For example, Norona refuses to participate in a group assignment. Her refusal seems to show disdain for the teacher, who thinks Norona is misbehaving. But Norona's reason for refusing is that she is intimidated by the prowess of her peers and doesn't want them to know she is inept. By refusing to participate, she hopes to hide her incompetence and avoid derision.

Suggestions: To help students such as Norona behave advantageously when faced with what they dislike, try the following:

- Ask students to tell what they try to avoid in school, such as people, events, or activities they find frightening and embarrassing.
- Ask which items on the list could best be dealt with through avoidance (e.g., a clique that is maligning other students), and which cannot be dealt with through avoidance (e.g., giving an oral report in front of the class). Select three or four that fall into different categories, such as things that are feared, disliked, embarrassing, demeaning, or provocative.
- For each of the conditions or situations, discuss the advantages and disadvantages of avoidance. For situations that must be confronted, ask students if they have ideas about how to do so successfully. For example, if Jayson is terrified of standing in front of the class and making a report, ask:

> "Is it possible to make a strength out of what appears to be a weakness? How might that be done?" (Perhaps using the extra motivation to advantage; perhaps admitting publicly that one is not very capable but is eager to learn from others.)
>
> "Can a person learn from situations that make them uncomfortable?" (Yes, often very desirable learning.)
>
> "What could a person do to reduce fear of the situation?" (Perhaps practice in pairs, then small groups, then large groups.)

Set up two or three scenarios involving avoidance and have students practice what to say and do in those situations.

7. *Regarding an egocentric personality*: Students with egocentric personalities focus on themselves, consider themselves superior to others, and believe they do no wrong. Most classes contain one or more such students.

Suggestions: To help these students behave more appropriately, ask in class discussions whether the needs and interests of all students are important, or whether only certain students deserve attention. Ask if one person is ever entirely right and the others entirely wrong, and if everyone is entitled to an equal opportunity.

As students answer, ask how teacher and class should react to a person who always wants to dominate, be first, be right, and quarrel with those who don't agree. Make sure the proffered suggestions are positive in nature, not negative.

Ask students if they think it would be a good idea to make a class agreement about equal opportunity, sharing, cooperating, and conducting oneself in a manner that does not antagonize others. This might all be incorporated in an agreement such as, "We will always treat others as we would like to be treated."

Causes that Originate in Class Peers and Groups

We saw in Chapter 9 that two significant causes of misbehavior originate in class peers and groups: provocation and group behavior. Here are suggestions for dealing with them.

8. *Regarding provocation*: A great portion of school misbehavior results from students being provoked by annoyance, insult, and boredom. Heather is trying to study but Roberto's incessant chatter frustrates her to the bursting point. Marty calls Jerry a name and Jerry responds hotly. Manuel is trying to pay attention but finally disengages from the lesson because he does not understand it and sees no point to it.

Suggestions: Provocation often produces strong emotions that reduce self-control and frequently increase combativeness. Discuss this phenomenon with your class. Ask whether provoking others is in keeping with the character the class is trying to build. Ask students to name some things people say or do that so upset them that they want to retaliate. Ask how they feel, and what they want to do, when someone steals from them, cheats them, abuses them, or subjects them to ridicule and teasing. Ask if retaliation is likely to improve the situation or make it worse. Ask what an offended student might do to defuse the incident.

Such discussions, coupled with practice, help students learn to maintain self-control and to act and speak more calmly when annoyed. Try asking students to think through situations such as the following:

- When someone has called you stupid or made you so angry you feel you must react, what can you do that will calm the situation, keep it from occurring again, and allow everyone to maintain his or her dignity?
- What do you sometimes do that provokes angry responses in others? Why do you do those things? How can you avoid them?
- If you find a lesson so boring you cannot pay attention, what should you do?

9. *Regarding group behavior*: Students often succumb to peer pressure or get caught up in group emotion. At those times, they may misbehave in ways they would never do if by themselves. It is difficult for students to disregard peer pressure, easy to get swept up in group energy and emotion, and easy to justify one's misbehavior as "only what others were doing." Because Kerry and Tomas want to look cool to their peers, Kerry defaces school property and Tomas bullies weaker members of the class, even though those acts are not what Kerry and Tomas would do if their peers were not present.

Suggestions: Address this phenomenon with your class using a discussion such as the following, adjusted to the maturity of your students.

- Tell the class about some event in which a friend of yours, let's say Sarah, behaved badly just because others were doing so. Indicate that Sarah is now very embarrassed about her behavior and wishes no one knew about it.
- Ask your students if they know any stories like Sarah's they can share, without mentioning names the class might recognize. If they share stories, guide

the class in analyzing one or two of them. If they don't contribute a story, have a fictional one ready for their consideration.

After hearing or recounting the story, ask questions such as:

- Is the behavior something the individual will be proud of later?
- Why do you suppose the individual behaved that way? (Perhaps fun, comradeship, testing limits, or being seen as clever or "cool.")
- What do you think the long-term results will be for the individual? (Perhaps an unpleasant story to remember, regret, guilt, getting caught, being found out, worry, disappointing one's parents, possible punishment, or living with knowing one did the wrong thing.)
- How do you think the benefits compare with the harmful effects?
- Once you do something you are ashamed of, is there any way to make amends?
- How can you stay away from, or keep out of, group activities that are unlawful, unethical, or against the rules?

QUESTIONS FOR SELF-IMPROVEMENT

1. Expediency was listed as a cause of misbehavior. Is there a positive side to expediency?

2. How many of the causes of misbehavior that originate in students are related to needs and failure to meet them? Which are they?

3. Would you say the following statement is true or false: "Most squabbles among class members are caused by provocation." Explain your answer.

ACTIVITIES FOR SELF-IMPROVEMENT

1. Examine the seven causes of misbehavior that originate in individual students. While they are known to promote misbehavior, do they have positive qualities as well? If so, what are they?

2. Of the seven causes of misbehavior that originate in individual students, which do you think you can reduce easily, and which do you think will present difficulties? Why?

3. Analyze your teaching behavior in terms of the first seven causes of misbehavior. How much does each of them affect your daily behavior in the classroom? Does any of them ever cause you to "misbehave" when teaching?

CHAPTER

11

Addressing Causes of Misbehavior that Originate in Instructional Environments and School Personnel

This chapter explains how to address causes of misbehavior that originate in instructional environments and school personnel. (The numbered items below continue causes of misbehavior listed in Chapter 10.) Causes that originate in environments are easy to deal with. Those that originate in adult personnel are more problematic, but they, too, can be addressed effectively.

Addressing Causes from Instructional Environments

Chapter 9 identified four causes of misbehavior that originate in instructional environments: physical discomfort, tedium, meaninglessness, and lack of motivation. These problems are easily corrected.

10. *Regarding physical discomfort*: Students are made restless or frustrated by inappropriate temperature, poor lighting, and uncomfortable seating and work spaces.
Suggestions: Attend to these factors in advance and ask students about them. Make changes as necessary.

11. *Regarding tedium*: Students begin to fidget after a time when an instructional activity requires continued close attention, especially if the topic is not particularly interesting.
Suggestions: Break the work into shorter segments or increase the interest level.

12. *Regarding meaninglessness:* Students grow restless when required to work at topics they do not comprehend or in which they see no purpose.
Suggestions: Make sure the topic is meaningful to students: that they understand it and see its relevance, importance, and applicability in their lives.

13. *Regarding lack of motivation*: Students have little interest in what they are expected to learn and, therefore, make little effort to learn it.

Suggestions: Emphasize topics and activities in which students have natural interest. When that is not possible, introduce elements students are known to enjoy, as described in Chapter 6.

Addressing Causes that Originate in School Personnel

Seven causes of misbehavior are attributable to school personnel. They include poor modeling, lack of personal attention, disregard for students' feelings, uninteresting lessons, ineffective guidance and feedback, poor communication, and coercion, threat, and punishment. These causes come mostly from teachers, but also from administrators, clerical staff, health personnel, cafeteria personnel, custodial personnel, and parents working in the school. The causes over which we have direct control are those that come from ourselves. They are the ones that receive attention here.

Teacher Misbehavior and Suggestions for Correcting It

At this point, let's take a moment to think about "teacher misbehavior." You have seen that teachers and other school personnel, by their attitudes and actions, often cause students to misbehave, but we have not explored the concept of teacher misbehavior per se.

We normally think of misbehavior as something only students do. Have you ever heard anyone say teachers misbehave? The very words seem preposterous, unless they refer to hanky-panky in the faculty lounge. But if, instead of saying teachers misbehave, suppose we say that, when teaching, they sometimes "behave inappropriately" or "behave negatively." There would be little argument.

Teachers are unusually dedicated, conscientious, and hardworking, and they care a great deal about their students. They don't receive the credit they deserve for these qualities. Yet, we know that some teachers, because of unfamiliarity with effective techniques or out of habit, frustration, or personal affront, occasionally do things that provoke conflict, inhibit student progress, and leave the class dispirited.

Because teachers know better than to do this and know how to avoid it, it is fair to call their actions misbehavior. If we are intent on improving behavior, we must address not only student misbehavior but teacher misbehavior as well.

Here are teacher misbehaviors that lead to student misbehavior. As a professional, make sure you never behave in these ways.

14. *Regarding presenting poor models of behavior*: We sometimes treat students with discourtesy or disregard. We are sometimes inconsistent, irresponsible, and lacking in self-control. We can't be perfect, but we must realize that when we treat students poorly—which is to say, in ways we would not want to be treated—we tear down what we have been trying to build. Imagine the effects on Mrs. Alexis's class when, after urging all students to speak respectfully to each other, she tells Misti and Roberta, "Sit down right now and keep your mouths shut!"

Suggestions: Always be the best model you can for your students, who watch you very closely and often conduct themselves as you do (especially when you misbehave). If you do anything inappropriate, you can expect before long to see your students do as you did.

15. *Regarding showing little interest in or appreciation for students*: We sometimes fail to show interest in students or appreciation for them as individuals, despite knowing that they want our attention and want us to be interested in their lives. When that happens, students become wary of us or they may disruptively seek the attention they desire.

At times we also forget the importance of helping students feel comfortable, motivated, and successful. If this happens often, and students are left feeling vulnerable and on their own, they lose trust in us.

Suggestions: Give each student as much personal attention as possible. Go out of your way to greet them, exchange a friendly word, show you are aware of their difficulties, try to help them feel at ease, and acknowledge their progress.

16. *Concerning disregarding students' feelings*: Some teachers teach autocratically with little regard for students' feelings. They order students about, point out their inadequacies, and speak to them sarcastically. The effects are hurtful and made worse when students think they are being treated unjustly. Students often respond by sulking and refusing to cooperate. Sometimes they talk back angrily and plot revenge.

Some teachers act as though they are blameless when students misbehave or fail to learn, and are eager to blame students for shortcomings. As we have noted, placing blame accomplishes nothing positive. Students who are made objects of blame never improve as a result. They look for, and often find, ways to retaliate against the teacher.

Suggestions: Remain alert to students' feelings not only of happiness and optimism, but also of distress, sadness, frustration, fear, boredom, and pessimism. Acknowledge their feelings considerately. Talk with students about them when it seems appropriate to do so. Show you understand and accept the emotions they are experiencing, and are ready to help if you can.

17. *Regarding presenting uninteresting lessons*: Students rally to us when we make our classes interesting, but they keep their distance when classes are dull. At times, all teachers feel like saying to students, "Here is the lesson and you know the expectations, so how about showing some responsibility and completing the assignments as you know you should." This feeling is understandable, but it never accomplishes anything positive. Nevertheless, some teachers, especially those suffering from burnout, try to teach this way.

Suggestions: Stay out of the dull lesson trap, which makes school stultifying for you and your students. Both of you enjoy engaging topics and appealing activities. Students want you to be enthusiastic, to have sparkle, and to behave attractively. You want them to be the same. School life is so much better under those conditions. Don't allow yourself to be a teacher who only goes through the motions while presenting a wooden curriculum.

18. *Regarding ineffective guidance and feedback*: Without proper guidance and feedback, students do not understand what to do or how to do it, and so remain inactive. When they do their work, they receive little sense of whether they have performed appropriately, what they have done well or poorly, how they could do better, or how much progress they have made. Under these circumstances, it is difficult for them to take their work seriously.

Suggestions: Make sure students understand clearly what they are supposed to do, how to do it, what they have done well or poorly, and how to improve. Verify their understanding by checking with them as a class and individually.

19. *Regarding communicating ineffectively*: Some teachers do not communicate well with students, even though they could do so easily. Students like you to exchange pleasantries with them. They want to know your views on things, and want to tell you theirs. They also want to know what is expected of them academically and how they are to conduct themselves. Students need personal communication from us: It is one of the main ways they receive personal validation.

Suggestions: Go out of your way to speak regularly with students in a friendly way. Avoid comments that hurt feelings or dampen enthusiasm. Say things that bolster their confidence. Build them up when you can. No need to fake it. You can find plenty of genuinely positive things to say to, and about, each of your students.

20. *Regarding coercion, threat, and punishment*: Students don't like to be made to do anything. They don't like to be threatened. They don't like to be punished. They react negatively to all these tactics, which make them drag their heels or sometimes refuse to participate. They keep an eye out for you, fearful of getting scolded, embarrassed, or demeaned. They often develop negative attitudes toward you and school and dream of getting away or taking revenge.

Suggestions: Give up coercion, threat, and punishment entirely. Replace them with considerate helpfulness, personal attention, and good communication. You can win student cooperation through kind treatment and personal enthusiasm. These days, students simply cannot be bullied into learning. You harm them and yourself when you try to use force.

The Causes of Teacher Misbehavior and How to Correct Them

We have been considering teacher misbehavior and the effects it has on students (and on teachers, too). We have not, however, identified what causes teachers to misbehave. Some of the main causes are presented here. If you recognize any of these in yourself, please consider the suggestions for correcting them.

1. *Habit*: Teachers sometimes become set in their ways of teaching and interacting with students. They may have learned their teaching style from their own teachers and, over the years, have remained comfortable with it.

Suggestions: Should this apply to you, watch closely to see how students react to you. Do they seem friendly? Afraid? Attracted to you? Eager to cooperate? Eager to please you? If they are reticent, fearful, hard to motivate, uncooperative, or unfriendly, analyze your teaching carefully and try to determine which of your behaviors might be causing trouble. Hold a discussion about teaching and ask students to tell about favorite teachers from the past. Pay attention to what they say and try adopting some of the characteristics or practices they like.

2. *Unfamiliarity with better techniques*: Some teachers have not had occasion to learn about newer, more effective ways of teaching and relating with today's students, ways that better promote desired learning, behavior, and attitudes.

Suggestions: Should this apply to you, ask other teachers about their favorite techniques in working with students. Scan professional journals that describe up-to-date practices. Use the vast resources available through the Internet. Read books that suggest better ways of working with students. Attend workshops on humane discipline, human relations, and character building.

3. *Frustration*: Some teachers get beaten down from continually having to deal with misbehavior. This leaves them stressed and makes it difficult for them to work with students in a kind, helpful manner.

Suggestions: If this applies to you, you are probably trying to force students to comply with your expectations and feel you are losing the battle of wills. You cannot teach happily in this way. Your frustration will disappear when your students become cooperative, willing to learn, and considerate toward each other and you. You can't force that to happen. You achieve it by removing the causes of misbehavior and enticing students with your attractive personality and interesting curriculum and style of teaching.

4. *Provocation*: Students sometimes do and say things, perhaps intentionally, to get under a teacher's skin. They hope to see the teacher get befuddled or lose self-control.

Suggestions: Should this apply to you, do not provoke your students, and do not allow yourself to be provoked by them. When they try, disregard their comments and actions and proceed as if nothing has happened. If you feel you must respond, only say, "I really regret you feel that way" or "What might I do that will make things better for you?" If they suggest you do something demeaning or dangerous, tell them, "I don't believe debasing or harming myself will make things better for you, but if you have a positive suggestion, please write it out for me and I'll consider it and see if we can work together. For now, I'd very much appreciate your cooperation in this lesson."

5. *Failure to plan proactively:* Many teachers do not think ahead sufficiently to foresee potential problems. They get caught by surprise and have difficulty saying or doing things that resolve the problems.

Suggestions: If this applies to you, think carefully about problems that might arise in class or reactions students might have to topics, lessons, your requests, or unexpected events. By anticipating potential difficulties, you can change you plans to keep the problems from arising, or you can prepare yourself to deal with whatever might eventuate. Verse yourself on what to do if you or a student is injured or becomes ill, if a student defies you, if students get into a fight, if an unauthorized visitor comes into the room, if a parent berates you, if the class moans when you make an assignment, and so forth. Determine how you can respond decisively to such situations, yet maintain positive relationships.

QUESTIONS FOR SELF-IMPROVEMENT

1. Which causes of misbehavior are easier to correct, those that originate in students or those that originate in yourself? Why?

2. Do you think it is fair to say teachers "misbehave" when we know they are almost always doing the best they can? Explain your thinking.

3. Do you think it is an overstatement to say, "Never use force or punishment when working with your students?" Can you think of times when force might be required? Can you think of times when punishment might be required?

4. This chapter refers to "school personnel" yet addresses the behavior of teachers, ignoring that of other adults at school. What do you think might be the rationale for that apparent inconsistency?

ACTIVITIES FOR SELF-IMPROVEMENT

1. Analyze yourself in terms of causes of student misbehavior that might be coming from you. Do you see any aspects of your personality, general behavior, or teaching style that might be at fault?

2. Consider the causes behind teacher misbehavior. Using yourself or a teacher you know, explain what might be done to remove factors that are causing you or the other person to misbehave professionally.

CHAPTER

12 Dealing with Misbehavior

This chapter describes more explicitly how to deal with misbehavior. It explains how to prevent misbehavior, support student self-control, and intervene productively when misbehavior occurs. Guidelines are provided to help you analyze and polish your own classroom behavior as well.

Discipline

The discipline process includes preventing misbehavior, supporting student self-control, and correcting misbehavior. Of these three functions, preventing misbehavior yields the greatest payoff. You should put strong effort into prevention, even though having to correct misbehavior probably worries you more. True, corrective discipline does present problems, but don't worry. You can handle them without undue difficulty, even the severe ones. Supporting student self-control is an intermediate position between prevention and correction. Easily managed, it helps students stay on-task and out of trouble when they first begin to grow edgy.

Preventing Misbehavior

Up to now, this book has been almost entirely about preventive discipline. It has urged you to do a number of things that eliminate potential discipline problems, such as:

- being friendly, helpful, and courteous to your students;
- validating your program in terms of student needs and your own;
- making curriculum and instruction as enjoyable as possible;
- collaborating with students by involving them to the extent possible;
- making collaborative agreements about class behavior and procedures;
- being the best model of ethical behavior you can;
- discussing with students class misbehavior, its effects, its causes, and how to avoid it;
- teaching students how to behave appropriately when necessary;
- providing situations that encourage students to cooperate with each other and assume responsible control over their behavior and learning;
- planning proactively to avoid potential problems and forestall misbehavior.

The final item in the list, proactive planning, was introduced in Chapter 2 and described further in Chapter 11. It involves thinking through in advance the events, conditions, situations, and behaviors that may occur in your classroom. This allows you to avoid many problems, reduce the seriousness of those that occur, and respond to all of them effectively. Another of the items in the list deals with establishing collaborative class agreements, which I explain further at this point.

Establishing Class Agreements

At the beginning of the class or semester, conduct a series of discussions with your students about curriculum and instruction, class procedures, and classroom behavior. Use these discussions to reach joint agreements that guide behavior in the class. Don't limit the agreements to student behavior, but extend them to teaching, treatment of students, and maintenance of good behavior in the class. Allow students to participate fully in developing the agreements. Their participation makes them likely to abide by the agreements, and it provides them a sense of responsibility and power. The process by which these agreements are reached is described in Chapter 15. Please check there if you wish more detail at this point.

Suppose you and your students have settled on the following agreements:

- We will always treat others as we would like them to treat us.
- We will make sure class activities are important and interesting.
- Our personal behavior will always be ethical, considerate, and responsible.
- We will keep the classroom orderly and comfortable.
- We will do high quality work we can be proud of.
- If anyone breaks these agreements, we will do what we can to help the person behave appropriately.

The agreements (note they are all positive in nature) should be printed and posted in the room, where they can be referred to and reviewed regularly.

Supporting Student Self-Control

You probably know that, toward the end of many lessons, some students begin to fidget, lose attention, glance out the window, or try to interact inappropriately with others. These actions tell you students are losing self-control, are on the verge of misbehaving, and need help in reestablishing self-control to complete the lesson. The help you provide at this point is called *supportive discipline.*

Here are some of the things you can do to support students' self-control. The results don't last long, but are effective for a few minutes.

- Use your charisma. Inject enthusiasm.
- Catch students' eyes. That refocuses them on work.
- Move alongside edgy students. Show interest in their work. Ask cheerful questions or make favorable comments.

- Sometimes provide a light challenge, such as, "Can you get five more of these done before time to stop?"
- Talk personally and helpfully with students inclined to misbehave.

Correcting Student Misbehavior

Despite your best efforts, you inevitably have to deal with misbehavior. At those times you need to intervene in a way that stops the misbehavior, gets the student back on track, and preserves positive feelings and relations. The way to make such interventions is to use the class agreements you and your students have established collaboratively. Those agreements not only indicate approved behavior but also how misbehavior should be addressed. To illustrate, suppose your class has agreed that, when anyone misbehaves, you the teacher will do one of the following:

- thank the person if he or she quickly stops;
- give the person a reminder that an agreement is being violated;
- point to a chart where the agreement is printed;
- have a private chat with the offender to see what can be done to help;
- ask the offender to do something nice for the offended;
- discuss it in a class meeting or private meeting with the student if it continues.

Now let's imagine a scenario in which Samuel taunts Maxim, usually the best student in class and somewhat full of himself, who has not done well on a test. This violates the class agreement about always treating others as we would like them to treat us. In accordance with the procedure students have helped formulate:

You look at Samuel. He doesn't stop, so you call his attention to the agreement he is breaking.

This alone almost always stops the misbehavior. However, in the unlikely event that Samuel keeps taunting Maxim, what should be done next?

Again use tactics the class has agreed to. You mention the violation to Samuel and remind him of the agreement. If that doesn't suffice, you say to him in a kindly way, "Samuel, what can I do to help you abide by our class agreement? Could we discuss this matter privately at (you name a time and place)? Perhaps you can make some suggestions." If that meeting occurs, try to understand what is causing the misbehavior and help Samuel see the undesirable effects of his misbehavior.

Effective Interventions

Intervention refers to your stepping in and dealing with misbehavior. Initiate the intervention by reminding the student of the class agreement and indicating acceptable behavior. If more is required, provide guidance, support, or direct instruction as needed. You should strive for the following during interventions. Discuss them with your class so they understand the emphasis on helpfulness rather than force.

- Be helpful and reasonable, never forceful or punitive.
- Take steps that make future transgressions less likely.
- Never be personally offensive or harmful.
- Allow positive relations to continue between you and the student.
- Help the offender save face, if possible, and maintain a positive attitude.

When you ask students what they think you should do when misbehavior occurs, their first suggestions are usually harsh, such as, "Make him stay in after class" or "Call her parents and tell them what she's done." At this point, help the class understand that good interventions provide assistance, not punishment. To clarify what you mean, ask questions such as:

- What are we hoping to accomplish with the intervention?
- Would doing what you suggest help the offender?
- How would the offender feel if treated this way?
- Would the intervention help or give comfort to any victims of the misbehavior?

Questions such as these may perplex students for a while, but before long they understand that the purpose of intervention is not just to stop the misbehavior, but also to help those who violate class agreements behave properly.

Following Through on Interventions

We hope that any intervention will make the student less likely to repeat the misbehavior. Toward that end, you need to make sure misbehaving students are fully aware of what they have done. You might ask them gently if they can help you understand why they behaved as they did. Give them ownership of the problem, and the responsibility for correcting it, by saying to them, "You have caused a problem for the class. How do you plan to resolve it?"

Barbara Coloroso (1999) suggests that, for more serious misbehavior, you may have to work with students to resolve the problem. In that process, the offending students should make restitution, and, if necessary, work toward reconciliation with others they have offended. By *resolution*, Coloroso means taking steps to identify and deal with the cause of the misbehavior. By *restitution*, she means the student's making right whatever he or she has done wrong. This involves a number of possibilities, such as replacing or repairing what has been damaged or helping restore the reputation of someone who has been wrongly degraded. This might involve learning to show more tolerance or curbing one's impulses. By *reconciliation*, Coloroso means making amends—smoothing things over with anyone who has been harmed or offended. This can be accomplished through sincere apology and doing something helpful for the offended person.

Patricia Kyle, Spencer Kagan, and Sally Scott (2001) have given additional attention to what students might do in the resolution phase. They advise teachers to talk with misbehaving students and together determine what triggers the disruptive behavior. Then teacher and students specify alternative behaviors that would be acceptable in similar situations. They call these alternatives "responsible choices." The misbehaving student practices responsible choices and applies them when appropriate. The teacher, meanwhile, keeps track of progress and, together with the student, evaluates the results.

You can decide, depending on the student and the situation, what kind of follow-up is needed. Some students need a great deal of help, while others don't need any. All in all, offending students should acknowledge they have misbehaved, accept responsibility for the misbehavior, take positive steps to correct it, make restitution or amends for any damage done, and consciously try to behave appropriately in the future.

How to Conduct Yourself during Interventions

When you intervene, do your best to remain calm and convey your desire to help, even if the student speaks to you disrespectfully. You might find it helpful to practice with a partner beforehand to improve your ability to:

- keep your composure when confronted with anger, hostility, or disrespect;
- hear, understand, and acknowledge the student's point of view;
- show continual willingness to help;
- carefully avoid using threat or punishment;
- seek to work together with the student to resolve the problem.

Also, be very careful that you never:

- react angrily;
- confront the student in a hostile manner;
- argue with the student;
- make demands, scold, moralize, or threaten the student's dignity;
- back the student into a corner;
- punish the student in any way.

Helping Students Abide By Class Agreements

We have noted that students are predisposed to abide by agreements they have helped create. By doing the following you can make their compliance still more likely.

- Regularly discuss the class agreements. Talk about how they are working, whether any of them needs to be modified, and whether any new ones are needed. Reaffirm their importance.
- Talk personally with individual students. Ask them if they are comfortable with the class, its standards, instruction, and the behavior of fellow students.
- Continually work with students to establish class character that reflects ethics, trust, dignity, helpfulness, responsibility, and joy.
- Conduct yourself in ways that model the best ethical behavior.
- Show students how to behave in stressful situations. Organize sessions in which they practice effective behavior in unpleasant circumstances. Teach

them how to respond positively to strong emotions such as fear, anger, jealousy, excitement, and frustration.

- Be alert for instances of exemplary student behavior. When you see them, express your admiration and appreciation.

Maintaining Your Own Appropriate Behavior

The very best teachers show exemplary behavior and are accessible, helpful, steadfast, and charismatic. We should continually strive for these five fabulous traits, which bring out the best in students. Here is what they entail.

Exemplary behavior.   Your behavior should be above reproach for two reasons: First, you teach behavior more by example than what you say. Second, you cannot expect students to behave with kindness, consideration, and responsibility when you yourself do not. The old "do as I say, not as I do" carries no weight with today's students.

Accessibility.   You must be available to your students if you hope to run a helpful, collaborative classroom. You must make time to talk with them on a personal basis, and you must be approachable. Students must not be afraid of you. They need to know they can speak with you openly when necessary and that you will not criticize or think harshly of them. This doesn't mean you should fraternize with students, but you do need to be available, open, and responsive.

Helpfulness.   You must always be helpful if you want students to cooperate with you and do their best. Helpfulness relieves you from being taskmaster–judge and allows you to serve as caretaker–facilitator. Students like this very much. They find little fault with teachers who are considerate and helpful.

Reliability.   You must be steadfast. Do not allow yourself to be accessible one day and aloof the next, or helpful one day and unconcerned the next. Things go better for everyone when you remain considerate and helpful, every day, all the time.

Charisma.   Finally, you need to be charismatic, at least to a degree. Charisma attracts students and makes them want to associate with you and imitate you. We noted earlier that some teachers don't show much charisma, a few almost none. Yet we all can acquire charisma by showing enthusiasm, taking personal interest in students, sharing aspects of family and personal life, revealing special talents, and maintaining a sense of humor (not silliness).

Analyzing Your Own Behavior

As a conscientious teacher, you will want to analyze your teaching style continually and how you relate with students continually. You can conduct this analysis alone or with a fellow educator you trust. Pay particular attention to:

- how you talk and relate with students;
- how students respond to you;
- how students react to the curriculum you provide;
- how students react to the instructional activities you use;
- the extent to which you involve students in making decisions and taking care of the class;
- your ability to maintain good behavior through helpfulness.

Correcting Errors in Your Behavior

Suppose your analysis identifies certain mistakes in your teaching style that you'd like to correct. How do you proceed? Here are some suggestions:

- *Apply the Fabulous Five.* Conscientiously apply the Five Fabulous Traits of outstanding teachers: exemplary behavior, accessibility, helpfulness, reliability, and charisma. Try to determine how to improve any of the five that fall short of what you desire.
- *Polish your teaching style.* Analyze your language, explanations, and ways of calling on students and providing feedback. Make sure what you say is to the point and helpful, and that it contains no sarcasm, putdowns, or signs of exasperation.
- *Keep yourself current.* Keep your eyes and ears open for the latest developments in working effectively with students.
- *If frustrated or stressed, deal with the cause, not the symptoms.* When frustrated in work, you can usually pinpoint the reasons for your malaise, which might be student lethargy, inattention, lack of respect, disruption, or failure to do acceptable work. You can address the causes of your distress by implementing the suggestions in this book. As you do so, your outlook will improve rapidly.
- *Don't provoke students or allow them to provoke you.* As mentioned earlier, make sure you don't provoke resistance and retaliation by the things you say and do, such as making unreasonable demands, treating students inconsiderately, or using language that is hurtful or threatening. If students try to provoke you, ask yourself why they do so. Think about their actions and your reactions. Instead of retaliating, remain calm and say something positive. As you show consideration and helpfulness, students lose interest in trying to make you lose your composure.
- *Think and plan proactively.* We have seen that the best teaching and discipline result from proactive planning, when you try to anticipate everything beforehand and decide how you will treat students and conduct yourself. This is not to say that spontaneity has no place in teaching. It is sometimes necessary and often effective. But generally you do better by thinking through the following in advance, as noted earlier in this chapter:
  - what will likely happen in given situations;
  - what you will say to students and ask them to do;
  - how they may react to your requests;
  - what you will say and do when they refuse to comply or talk back.

As you plan, think also about how you communicate and respond. This will help you say and do things that are beneficial to you and your students.

Admitting Your Mistakes

Sometimes you will violate class agreements. Usually you will know immediately when you have done so. If not, students will call it to your attention, either directly or by the expressions on their faces. At that time stop what you are doing and admit your mistake. Simply say you realize what you have done and know it is a violation of class expectations. Apologize to whomever has reason to be offended. Admit your culpability, express your regret, indicate you hope never to do it again, and ask students to help you guard against future transgressions.

QUESTIONS FOR SELF-IMPROVEMENT

1. In your own words, can you explain the meanings of *preventive discipline, supportive discipline,* and *corrective discipline?* Can you give an example of what you might say or do in performing each one?

2. What is the value of proactive planning in preventing misbehavior? In dealing with misbehavior that occurs?

3. What role do class agreements play in helping you intervene effectively in misbehavior?

4. What is the single most important quality you should emphasize when working with students?

ACTIVITIES FOR SELF-IMPROVEMENT

1. Describe yourself in terms of the "fabulous five" traits of effective teachers. How do you rate in each?

2. Analyze your teaching style as it is, or as you think it would be given your philosophy and personality. How do you describe yourself? How might you increase your effectiveness?

3. Suppose you are taking your class on a field trip to a local business. Indicate five important things you should anticipate and plan for. Tell how you would deal with those five things, before or after they might happen.

4. Suppose Mr. Tomalat asks you to punish his son Umil if he conducts himself improperly at school. Compose a reply to Mr. Tomalat that will satisfy him and keep him on your side.

PART FIVE

Strengthening Your Class

Part 5 examines strategies for improving the class in ways that allow learning to occur more effectively and pleasantly. We begin by exploring class character, what it is, how it affects behavior, and how it can be appraised and strengthened. From there we move ahead to improving class communication and human relations. We then see how to introduce and implement Helpful Discipline in the classroom. A final chapter summarizes the nature, value, and procedures of Helpful Discipline.

CHAPTER

13 Strengthening Class Character

This chapter explores the nature of class character and the effects it has on discipline. Class character, which can be thought of as the personality of the class, is comprised of a number of individual qualities. Those qualities are identified, a guide is provided for appraising them, and suggestions are made for strengthening them.

The Nature of Class Character

We said earlier that classes have distinct personalities, just as individuals do. Some are happy and outgoing, some serious and hardworking, some boorish, lethargic, and aimlessly chaotic. These personalities are outward manifestations of class character.

Character strongly affects discipline. In classes that are positive and helpful, little misbehavior occurs. Students learn rapidly and enjoy themselves in the process. But in classes that are aimless or negative, students misbehave frequently. They make little progress and find little pleasure in school.

The Components of Class Character

Class character is comprised of thirteen separate qualities. Each of the qualities is present in every class in degrees varying from weak to strong. The stronger the individual qualities, the stronger the overall class character. In most classes, some of the qualities are strong while others are weak. Observe any class and you can fairly easily note the qualities and their relative strength. Here are the thirteen qualities:

1. *Ethics*—right and wrong ways of conducting oneself and treating others, especially with regard to kindness, honesty, and fairness
2. *Trust*—having confidence in others, that they will do the proper thing, won't harm you, and will help in times of need
3. *Consideration*—recognizing the individuality of other people and interacting with them in keeping with their needs, traits, and personal circumstances
4. *Dignity*—respect assigned to ourselves and others as people of competence and value
5. *Personal power*—the ability and opportunity to influence others and control certain aspects of our lives
6. *Opportunity*—access for all class members to important learning and the tools and materials required
7. *Purposefulness*—having a clear idea of what we want to achieve, why and how to go about it
8. *Persistence*—sticking with tasks and following them through to completion, even when they are difficult and frustrating
9. *Responsibility*—taking on tasks, carrying them out to the best of our ability, showing reliability and self-control, and being willing to accept the results of our actions
10. *Energy*—the presence of high levels of motivation and activity
11. *Helpfulness*—willingly assisting others when the need is present
12. *Collaboration*—teachers and students working together cooperatively to make progress and resolve difficulties
13. *Joy*—the sense of happiness and satisfaction

You might want to display this list in your classroom so you can refer to it and discuss the qualities with your students.

Appraising Class Character

You assess the character of your class by appraising the thirteen qualities. Those qualities are evident in the ways students and teachers conduct themselves, how purposefully they work, and how much they enjoy the process. Here are criteria you can use for judging the character of your class and determining which qualities require attention:

- *Regarding ethics*: Class members treat each other kindly, honestly, and fairly.
- *Regarding trust*: Class members are comfortable with the teacher and each other, confident of being treated in a kind and helpful manner.
- *Regarding consideration*: Class members show concern for each other's feelings, comfort, and dignity.
- *Regarding dignity*: Class members are considerate of each other and treat each other with courtesy and respect.
- *Regarding personal power*: Class members have frequent opportunities to make decisions, assume responsibilities, and plan their own activities.
- *Regarding opportunity*: Class members have abundant opportunity to participate, learn, and use instructional materials.
- *Regarding purposefulness*: Class members have clear notions of what they are to accomplish, why it is important, and how they are to proceed.
- *Regarding persistence*: Class members work diligently, do not give up easily, and strive for quality.
- *Regarding responsibility*: Class members pursue tasks, complete them satisfactorily in accordance with existing conditions, accept credit or blame for the results, and make corrections or recompense when necessary.
- *Regarding energy*: Class members show a high level of purposeful activity when it is appropriate to do so.
- *Regarding helpfulness*: Class members routinely offer to help others in need.
- *Regarding collaboration*: Teacher and students work together toward the goals of education in a manner each considers productive and enjoyable.
- *Regarding joy*: A sense of pleasure and satisfaction pervades the class.

Strengthening Class Character

Your appraisal may reveal qualities of your class that you wish to strengthen. The following pages suggest how that can be done. Keep in mind that we build the qualities in individual students. As individual student character grows stronger, so does class character.

Strengthening Ethics

Classroom ethics include kindness, honesty, and fairness: treating people well and doing the right thing. Students may not be overly ethical when you first begin working with them, but they are ever watchful to make sure you are.

Kindness is best expressed in the Golden Rule: treating others as we, ourselves, want to be treated. No one wants to be disrespected, derided, or treated coldly. Students need to learn that kindness makes those feelings less likely and is the key to good relationships.

Honesty means being truthful with oneself and others in all matters of consequence. It requires keeping one's word, refusing to cheat and lie, admitting mistakes and failures, and never resorting to deceit. Draw students into exploring the benefits of behaving honestly, even when doing so produces temporary discomfort. Help them to see the difference between dishonesty and making mistakes and to understand that, while mistakes are a natural and beneficial part of learning, dishonesty can destroy trust and is never forgotten.

Fairness means treating others with as much wisdom and even-handedness as possible. You may grow tired of hearing your students say, "That's not fair," but you can use it as an opportunity to ask them what they think *fairness* means. This can lead to discussions about whether students want to be treated always the same or in accordance with their needs and circumstances at a given time.

Strengthening Trust

Trust means having strong confidence in others. None of us likes to work with people we think might renege on commitments or run us down behind our backs, whereas we feel secure with people who are ethical and reliable.

Trust develops naturally when the class operates on ethical principles and teachers show genuine concern for students. To encourage trust, you and your students must commit yourselves to behavior that is kind, honest, and fair. Trust grows slowly among students who are wary. You can establish it if you persevere, but be warned: It is easily lost, much more quickly than it is gained. A single violation of ethics can wipe out trust that has taken weeks to build. As Stephen Covey reminds us:

> People will forgive mistakes, because mistakes are usually of the mind, mistakes of judgment. But people will not easily forgive the mistakes of the heart, the ill intention, the bad motives, the prideful justifying cover-up of the first mistake (1989, p. 199).

Here are some things you and your students can do to build trust in your class. Discuss them with students as you feel appropriate.

- Listen to each other carefully and take each other seriously.

- Recognize and appreciate the uniqueness of each person.
- Speak kindly with others, in a supportive tone of voice.
- Never intentionally deceive others, or harm or slight them.
- Draw attention to others and give credit where it is due.
- Do not expect others to be perfect; make allowance for their imperfections and ask them to make allowance for yours.

Strengthening Consideration

Consideration means sensitively recognizing and showing tolerance for other people's beliefs, attitudes, values, and needs. People want to be accepted and treated with kindness. Sometimes they need encouragement, sometimes sympathy, sometimes support. Always they need tolerance. To strengthen consideration in your classes, do two things: First, always treat students considerately. Second, in class discussions ask questions that make students think about consideration, such as:

- Think of a time when your feelings were really hurt. How did you want to be treated at that time?
- Think of a time when you felt quite out of place because you were among people different from yourself. How did you feel? How did you want to be treated? How do you think you should have acted toward them?
- How can we tell when others are feeling ill at ease or worried or hurt? What do you see that tells you?
- What do you think it means to be considerate of others? How do you act when being considerate?
- Why do you think it is important for all of us to be considerate of each other? What does it do for us personally? For fellow students? For the class as a whole?

Strengthening Dignity

Dignity, or self-respect, grows stronger as we become more competent and feel valued and respected by others. One of the most powerful ways to influence students is to help them acquire dignity. We can do this in several ways, by showing we admire and value them, by drawing positive attention to them, by mentioning things they have accomplished, by treating them courteously, and by asking their opinions and listening to what they say.

When we treat students in these ways, they begin to seek us out, ask our advice, and cooperate with us. They give us a great bonus in return: They confer dignity on us, by showing respect and even affection. Help your students understand that, if they want to build a solid reputation for themselves, the best way to do so is by being ethical, showing respect for others, and mentioning others' positive qualities. Encourage them to practice those things when relating with each other. Be alert for such behavior and, when you see it, mention it favorably in class.

Strengthening Personal Power

Personal power is strengthened when we are allowed to make choices, make decisions, and assume control of certain aspects of our lives. When you empower your students in these ways, they begin to feel more in control of themselves and better able to deal with what life brings. You can provide this sense of power and strengthen it in a number of ways, such as:

- treating your students as social equals;
- asking for and listening to their opinions;
- allowing them to make choices about how they will work, what they will try to accomplish, and how they will show evidence of accomplishment;
- involving them as partners in planning class matters;
- taking their views into account and building on them;
- assigning them responsibilities in maintaining the well-being of the class;
- allowing them to be self-directing in undertaking and completing tasks or projects;
- encouraging them to accept responsibility for the outcomes of their efforts, whether those outcomes are good or bad; this helps them understand that their decisions have consequences;
- allowing them to try to correct or make amends for mistakes.

Students will make mistakes when exercising power. Make it possible for them to deal with those mistakes in a positive way. Help them see that power over others can be helpful or hurtful, depending on how it is used.

Strengthening Opportunity

Opportunity refers to all students having the continuing option of engaging in activities that lead to important learning. You make this happen by ensuring that a variety of learning possibilities are always open to students and that everyone has access to them. Work with students to establish a democratic classroom where everyone helps plan class life. Allow students to undertake projects in groups or on their own, but ask them to make a plan for what they will do and how they will show progress. You can help them find needed resources and you can show them how to evaluate their work and the overall experience.

Strengthening Purposefulness

Purposefulness means knowing clearly what we want to accomplish and how to go about it. We have noted that many students, by the time they reach the secondary years, don't see much point in attending school. They have lost hope it will offer them anything of value, so they stop trying.

You can help students grasp a sense of purpose in school, and in their lives, by doing the following: (1) Allow them to identify and pursue topics they truly want to learn about; (2) ask them to plan what they hope to accomplish, how they will go about it, what resources they will need and where to get them, and what evidence will tell them they have accomplished their intentions; (3) talk with them about obstacles they may encounter and satisfactions they can anticipate in the process.

Strengthening Persistence

Persistence is strengthened as we help students stick with tasks to completion, even when the tasks are difficult and frustrating. While persistence in the face of unfavorable conditions is a quality much admired, we get better results in school by allowing persistence to occur naturally in response to interesting curriculum and engaging teaching. Here are some suggestions.

- Provide an interesting, worthwhile curriculum and teach it well.
- Provide a warm, supportive, helpful class climate.
- If students are expected to pursue topics they don't enjoy, explain convincingly why the topics are necessary and devise ways of making them interesting.
- Help students see the advantages of doing the best work they can. Teach them the process for doing quality work, which involves evaluating their own work, improving it, and, after that, trying to find ways to improve it still further. Students may resist this process at first, but over time they come to enjoy it.

Strengthening Responsibility

Responsibility is strengthened when we

- undertake important tasks;
- make decisions and behave in accordance with expectations;
- complete tasks satisfactorily given existing conditions;
- accept the results of our efforts whether they bring success, failure, excellence, mediocrity, compliments, or criticism;
- acknowledge that we have played the major role in producing the results, whatever they may be;
- evaluate our efforts with an eye to making future improvements.

Strengthening Energy

There are a number of ways to increase class energy. Interesting curriculum, enjoyable activities, considerate relationships, enthusiasm, and teacher charisma all contribute. A sense of class purpose is especially energizing when it involves working together with others to complete a project, put on a performance, or compete against another class. Class synergy, in which students feed energy to each other, produces high levels of motivation (Charles, 2000). So do both cooperation and competition. Cooperation produces enjoyment and quantity and divergence of ideas, while competition produces motivation, independent thought, responsibility, and efficiency. (However, remember that competition can also demoralize those who never have a chance of winning. It can also cause them to lie and cheat in attempting to win.)

When appropriate, find ways for students to work cooperatively in groups or teams, especially in competition against other groups. This gives everyone a stake in the outcome and produces very high levels of energy.

Margarita Carlos, a middle school teacher in California, provides this anecdote that illustrates the energy levels of thirteen-year-old students when involved in activities they enjoy.

> This year on the day before Spring Break I let my students have a talent show and I filmed them on video. You would have thought I was giving them money, they were so excited. Among the 'talents' they shared were wrestling in the World Wrestling Federation style, saying words with burps, arching eyebrows, singing a cappella, lip syncing and dancing to a current song, performing like rock stars using lacrosse sticks as guitars, doing impersonations of teachers, dancing, juggling, and singing little children's songs in a big group. I'm not sure how I would justify all that educationally, but, let me tell you, my students sure enjoyed it, and it gave me an opportunity to understand them in contexts other than lessons and paper-and-pencil work.

Strengthening Helpfulness

Helpfulness refers to your providing assistance to students and to members of the class willingly assisting each other, including you, when the need is present. Helpfulness is strengthened as you and your students sense each is cared about and, in turn, come to care about each other.

Earlier we noted Haim Ginott's (1972) contention that teachers have a hidden asset they can always count on, which is looking for ways to be most helpful to students at any given time. He would have you always ask yourself, "What can I do to help my students right now." When students misbehave or get stuck in their work, you can ask them directly, "What can I do to help you?" Once the class commits itself to helpfulness, much of the misbehavior disappears.

Strengthening Collaboration

You can strengthen collaboration by drawing students into genuine partnership with you to make all aspects of class life pleasurable and rewarding. Consult with students and involve them however you can in

- making curriculum and instruction enjoyable and satisfying;
- meeting students' and the teacher's needs;

- living by the Golden Rule;
- removing or reducing the known causes of misbehavior;
- showing consideration and accepting responsibility;
- planning the discipline system;
- enhancing class character;
- establishing quality in all aspects of the school experience.

Strengthening Joy

Joy is a prevailing sense of happiness and satisfaction, a quality many students claim they don't often experience in school. It grows when students pursue topics they find fascinating, participate in enjoyable activities, and associate with teachers and fellow students who are trustworthy and engaging. Teacher enthusiasm and charisma add greatly.

As you work with students, provide examples and do demonstrations that keep the class lively. Communicate with students on a one-to-one basis. Inject humor as appropriate. Encourage students to look for what is fun, intriguing, or exciting in class activities and new learning. Never use sarcasm, denigrate students, or put them on the defensive. If you are unhappy about what is happening in the class, discuss your concerns with the students and find out if, together, you can work things out.

QUESTIONS FOR SELF-IMPROVEMENT

1. Of the thirteen qualities that comprise class character, which two do you consider most important to good education, and which two least important? Can you think of other qualities you would add to the list? Any you would delete?

2. The chapter implies that students will see personal advantage in developing stronger class character. To what extent do you think this implication is realistic? What might work against it? Could the counterforces you identify (if any) be neutralized?

3. To what extent do you think individual qualities of trust, dignity, and purposefulness change with circumstances? Can the qualities be strengthened and made relatively permanent, or must they be reestablished anew as students change from class to class or teacher to teacher?

4. Looking back, can you identify one of your teachers who tried to strengthen class character? If so, what did he or she do in that regard?

ACTIVITIES FOR SELF-IMPROVEMENT

1. Indicate how you would help students understand the reciprocal relationship in which individual student character affects class character and, in turn, class character affects individual character?

2. Select one of the qualities that comprise class character. In no more than one page, indicate how you would work with students to strengthen that quality.

3. For many years, teachers were urged to use an instructional style called "direct teaching" in which they carefully planned all instructional activities, directed students through them step-by-step, ensured that students remained constantly on-task, and evaluated lesson effectiveness in terms of student performance on tests. Which qualities of class character do you think might be strengthened by direct teaching, and which do you think might be harmed?

4. In accordance with the criteria for appraising class character, evaluate the character of a class you know about, perhaps your own or one you have worked in or observed.

14 Strengthening Communication and Human Relations

This chapter offers suggestions for improving communication and human relations in your classes. Communication, as the term is used here, refers to speaking with others in ways that foster goodwill. Human relations have to do with how we treat each other. We have already given much attention to helpfulness, consideration, ethics, and abiding by the Golden Rule. Here you will see additional ways of interacting with others to build strong personal relationships.

Strengthening Communication

How we speak to others greatly affects behavior, quality of learning, and enjoyment in the classroom. Usually, when we say communication, we are referring to exchanges of ideas, but here focus is placed on another aspect of communication that is even more important in discipline. It has to do with speaking in ways that show consideration and support for others and validates them as individuals. If you give attention to this function of communication, you will help students get along better and cooperate with you and each other. You will find three techniques especially helpful: using congruent communication, avoiding roadblocks, and using builders rather than barriers.

Using Congruent Communication

Congruent communication means saying things that are helpful to students while harmonious with their feelings about situations and themselves. The concept, popularized by Haim Ginott (1972), addresses misbehavior and accidents without embarrassing students or putting them on the defensive. Instead of saying, "Well, I see you've made a mess" (a hurtful statement that does little to help students use better judgment), you might pleasantly say, "Can you get that cleaned up before the bell rings?"

Teachers at their best, Ginott said, do not preach, moralize, impose guilt, or demand promises.Instead, they confer dignity on their students by treating them as social equals capable of making good decisions. Teachers at their worst label students, belittle them, and denigrate their character. They usually do these things inadvertently, unaware of the detrimental effect on students.

As you practice congruent communication, remember that it makes no use of "why" questions that carry blame, such as "Why didn't you finish this work? Why am I having to tell you again?" Instead, it would use an alternative such as, "When do you think you can have the work completed?"

It avoids moralistic lectures such as "You are not making an effort . . . You will never get anywhere in life . . . ," etc. A suitable alternative is, "Have another try. Let's see what you can do."

It does not use caustic or sarcastic remarks, such as "How odd; that's the fourth time you've lost your assignment." A congruent statement might be, "It is important that this work be done well. When do you think you will have it?"

It does not deny students' feelings with statements such as, "You are too big to cry" or "You have absolutely nothing to worry about." A suitable alternative would be, "I can see this is troubling you quite a bit."

It does not demand student cooperation, such as by saying, "Get back in your seat and get to work. It's time you carried your end of the load." A suitable alternative would be, "I could really use your help."

In congruent communication, you never lose your temper or self-control and say things such as, "Once and for all, sit down and keep your mouth shut!" A suitable alternative would be to breathe deeply, say nothing for a few seconds, and then say, "Let's think for a moment about agreement number 3 on our list."

Congruent communication holds that one of the best ways to correct misbehavior is simply to remind students how to behave properly. This is done most effectively through *I-messages,* as distinct from *you-messages.* An I-message might be, "I feel the noise level is a bit too high." A you-message might be, "You are so noisy nobody can think." I-messages tell how you feel personally about the situation, while you-messages attack or blame the student.

Avoiding Roadblocks

When students are worried or have difficulty with their work, you naturally try to help them. Yet, in doing so you might say things that push students away from you. Thomas Gordon (1989) has written at length about such communication errors, which he calls "roadblocks to communication." Examples of roadblocks are:

> *Giving orders.* ("Get busy. Don't waste any more time.")
> *Warning.* ("I'm telling you for the last time to get to work. If you don't, you'll be taking that home with you tonight along with a note to your parents.")
> *Preaching.* ("You need to complete this work. It's for your own good, don't you see that? If you can't do this you are never going to be an educated person.")
> *Advising.* ("Let me give you a piece of advice you will benefit from. I'd like to see you follow it.")
> *Criticizing.* ("I can't believe you are fooling around again. You have ability but you are not using it. I'm really disappointed in you.")

Questioning. ("What's the matter? Why aren't you getting this done? What's troubling you?")

When teachers use such comments and question, they tend to shut off communication and frequently make students feel worse and less inclined to work. Think for a moment how you speak with students. If you are using any of these roadblocks, consider replacing them with comments such as:

- "Many people have trouble getting started. That happens to me, too. Is there anything I can do to help?"
- "Is there something about the assignment that bothers you? Tell me what it is, if you can, and I'll try to correct it."
- "I feel something is bothering you. I don't want to pry. If you feel like talking, I'll listen now or I'll be here in the room right after school."

Using Builders rather than Barriers

Jane Nelsen, Lynn Lott, and H. Stephen Glenn (2000) have identified other things teachers do or say that affect students positively or negatively. They call comments that have positive effects "builders." Builders are respectful and encouraging. They call comments with negative effects "barriers." Barriers are disrespectful and discouraging. Here are examples.

Assuming versus Checking.
Barrier: Assuming. You assume, without checking with students, that you know what they are thinking and feeling, or what they can and cannot do, or how they should or should not respond. You deal with them on the basis of those assumptions.
Builder: Checking. Check with your students about what they think and feel. "Are you tired?" "Can you do some more?" "Are you enjoying this?" Then proceed on the basis of what they say.

Rescuing/Explaining versus Exploring.
Barrier: Rescuing and explaining. You try to help students by making lengthy explanations, getting them out of difficulties, or helping them do their work.
Builder: Exploring. Allow students to perceive situations for themselves and proceed on the basis of those perceptions. "Do you think you can do this on your own?" "I think you see what to do." "You understand the problem, now let's see what you can do."

Directing versus Inviting/Encouraging.
Barrier: Directing. You find yourself constantly telling students what to do. "Would you pick that up?" "Would you put that away?" "Make sure your desks are straightened out before the bell rings."
Builder: Encouraging. Encourage students to become self-directed. You might say, "The bell will ring soon. I would appreciate anything you might do to help get the room straightened up."

Adult-isms versus Respecting.

Barrier: Adult-isms. You use adult-isms that produce shame or guilt. These are usually questions that indicate what you want students to do, such as: "How come you never . . . ?" "Why can't you ever . . . ?"

Builder: Respecting. Show respect for students. Instead of handing back an unacceptable paper and saying, "You knew what I wanted on this project!" you could say, "What is your understanding of the requirements for this project?"

Strengthening Human Relations

Human relations have to do with how we treat each other in various situations. When using good human relations, we deal with each other in ways that satisfy everyone. We want to treat Mary well, and want her to treat us the same. We want Alberto and Reynald to speak kindly and show consideration for each other. We want to know what causes friction in the class and how to minimize it. We may need to teach students about good manners, which can be explained to them as ways of showing kindness to others. We may want to help students see the importance of giving others their full attention. We want them to know how to make a good impression and be nice people with whom to associate and work. And we want them to know how to resolve conflicts productively.

Specific Things We Try to Accomplish

Consider encouraging your students to discuss and practice the following skills in situations where they feel safe and don't mind making mistakes or appearing foolish.

Making a good impression.   When we make a good impression, others are more inclined to have dealings with us. Yet many of us don't make good first impressions. When you first meet someone, the best thing to do is smile, say your name clearly, and memorize the other person's name. Then, using the person's name, say something cordial or interesting.

Opening up communication.   Some people are able to communicate with strangers at the drop of a hat while others find it very difficult. Those who need help can profit from practice in using builders together with empathetic listening, which is discussed later in this chapter. For example, you can ask a question about a current event, and, when the other person responds, make comments to keep the exchange going. Depending on the topic, such comments might be: "Interesting. Tell me more about it." "What do you think we'd have to do if we tried something like that? Would it be possible?" "I've never worked on anything like this. How could we make it happen?" As the other person speaks further, listen carefully in order to grasp not only what is being said, but what it seems to mean to the person.

Conferring dignity.   One of the most powerful techniques we have for encouraging others to treat us well is to confer dignity on them. As previously noted, we do this by showing interest, remembering and using their names, mentioning something notable we have learned about them, treating them courteously, asking their opinion, listening to them, and acknowledging their contributions. This should be done from a position of social equality, otherwise our positive comments sound patronizing or fawning. Many people never seem to understand that they cannot gain stature through domineering, behaving subserviently, or gossiping and running others down.

Using positive body language.   One of the most powerful means for conveying feelings to others is body language. We all use body language when communicating, but are relatively unaware of doing so. It consists of physical mannerisms such as facial expressions, eye contact, gestures, and body posture and proximity. If what you are saying with words seems different from what you are saying with your body, the body message carries the stronger impact. The old saying about actions speaking louder than words holds true in all human interactions. You are more likely to understand what a person is really feeling or saying by interpreting voice sounds and body language than by interpreting speech verbatim.

Reacting positively to others.   Suppose someone is sharing information with you. You want to remain on good terms with the individual, so how should you react to what he or she says? If his or her contentions sound crazy, should you say so?

Yes, but not in so many words. Use some tact. You can say, "Tell me more about that," or "You know, that idea is new to me. Could you explain it a bit further?" If you disagree with what the person says, you can give your opinion gently, saying something like, "I may be wrong, but I have thought about it a bit differently," and then express your view. Saying "I may be wrong . . . " is one of the best ways to disagree with others. It lessens their defensiveness and keeps them open to your opinion.

What You Should Be Sure *Not* To Do

Here are some of the things you should be sure *not* to do or use when relating with others:

Slights.   If you want to get along with others, never slight them. Give them your full attention and the credit they are due.

Putdowns.   Don't make disparaging remarks about, or to, others. Don't speak sarcastically and then laugh as though you didn't mean it. The message is that you meant exactly what you said. Don't mention others' failures or shortcomings. You gain nothing by doing so, while there is a good chance you will lose their cooperation and good will.

Sarcasm.   Sarcasm can, at times, be delightfully funny, provided it is not directed at us, but it never improves personal relations. Even we adults have trouble learning that, so how can we expect students to do so without some help? You need to teach students that sarcasm hurts feelings. It doesn't matter whether it is done with words or by mannerisms such as rolling the eyes or snickering. Teach students that sarcasm is a way of trying to make yourself look superior to others. It is dangerous and it doesn't work.

Handling Problems and Conflicts

Problems and conflicts have much in common. Both involve a difficulty or an obstacle. They differ in that problems seldom pit one person or side against another, and the emotions are not intense. In resolving problems, everyone can work together harmoniously toward the same end. Conflicts, however, bring combativeness and emotionality, with each side trying to outdo the other.

Problems.   Many troublesome situations involve a difficulty everybody wants to see resolved. The "discipline problem" is a good example. The class might experience problems such as tardiness, wasted time, or criticism from an administrator. The usual procedure for resolving the problem would be for you to assess the problem (from your viewpoint) and tell the class how to correct it. Helpful Discipline operates a bit differently. It involves the class in a problem-solving procedure:

Step 1. Ask the class to help clarify the problem. Try to state exactly what is occurring, who it is bothering, and why it is troublesome.

Step 2. Use brainstorming to identify possible solutions. Involve everyone. Listen to all ideas. List suggestions on the board or a chart.

Step 3. Ask the class to discuss the suggested solutions and select one that seems likely to produce the desired results.

Step 4. Try the proposed solution. See how it works in practice. Modify it or move to another option if necessary.

Conflicts.   Conflicts are strong disagreements involving clashes of wills that make those involved feel threatened. Emotions run high. Both sides try to "win" and protect themselves against loss of dignity. Unless individuals have been trained to resolve conflicts productively, each struggles verbally to prove he or she is in the right.

Conflict resolution is done differently in Helpful Discipline: We try to find a solution that helps both sides be mostly correct or get most of what they want. This strategy is known by various names, such as "win/win conflict resolution" and "no-lose conflict resolution." In the absence of win/win resolution, conflicts usually conclude with one side "winning" and the other side "losing." For example, Ms. Allison and student Jerry have an emotional disagreement over the grade Jerry received on his theme. Jerry, highly motivated to receive good grades, complains.

Ms. Allison justifies the grade and decides not to change it. In this case Ms. Allison "wins" and Jerry "loses." That would be the end of the matter, except that Jerry, because he didn't get what he badly wanted, harbors a smoldering resentment against Ms. Allison.

In win/win conflict resolution, both sides end up feeling all right about the outcome. If Ms. Allison were enlightened in conflict resolution, she would listen carefully to Jerry's complaint. She would indicate she understands his contentions, but feels her grade is justified and would explain why. If Jerry still feels he has been wronged, Ms. Allison now might ask, "I wonder what we might do so I can maintain my standards and you can have an opportunity to receive the grade you want? Do you have any suggestions?" She and Jerry discuss options. They settle on a solution in which Jerry agrees to rewrite the theme, strengthening the weaknesses Ms. Allison has identified. This gives Jerry an opportunity for a good grade, though receiving one is still not a certainty, and Ms. Allison does not feel she has abandoned her integrity.

Benefits of win/win conflict resolution are threefold: Damage to personal egos is minimized, thus preserving positive working relationships; motivation is maintained—work continues with no sulking; and dignity is preserved for everyone. Once people learn to use this process, they can apply it in many life matters. In a nutshell, the win/win process is done as follows:

1. Both disputants identify and explain their primary concerns.
2. Each disputant listens carefully and tries genuinely to see the situation from the other's point of view.
3. Through discussion, the disputants identify possible solutions that seem acceptable to both.
4. A solution is implemented and good relations are maintained.

By listening carefully to others, we can also "get inside their heads" and see past their words to their underlying hopes, fears, realities, and difficulties. This is what is meant by "empathetic listening," referred to earlier in this chapter. Stephen R. Covey describes it as follows:

> If I were to summarize in one sentence the single most important principle I have learned in the field of interpersonal relations, it would be this: *Seek first to understand, then to be understood*. This principle is the key to effective interpersonal communication (1989, p. 237).

Covey further reminds us:

> Empathetic listening takes time, but it doesn't take anywhere near as much time as it takes to back up and correct misunderstandings when you're already miles down the road, to redo, to live with unexpressed and unsolved problems . . . People want to be understood. And whatever investment of time it takes to do that will bring much greater returns of time as you work from an accurate understanding of (their) problems and issues . . . (1989, p. 253).

By following Covey's advice on understanding others' feelings as well as their points of view, you can defuse confrontations and prevent emotions from becoming so inflamed that neither disputant can listen to reason or consider compromise. Linda Albert (1996) provides further advice on how to conduct yourself in conflict discussions:

1. *Keep focus on the behavior, not the other person.* In the conflict between Ms. Allison and Jerry, the enlightened Ms. Allison would focus on the work, not Jerry. She would not blame him. She would simply point out areas of his work that were not as strong as they should have been.

2. *Deal with the moment.* Keep the discussion focused on the matter at hand right now. Neither Jerry nor Ms. Allison brings up anything the other might have done in the past.

3. *Take charge of your negative emotions.* If you are involved in a conflict, it is very possible that your feelings will get hurt, but you must not become combative. You can reduce the other's desire to fight by responding calmly and objectively, keeping your voice moderated, avoiding finger-pointing or -wagging, and not thinking you must have the last word.

4. *Allow the other person to save face.* Instead of trying to make Jerry knuckle under, Ms. Allison calmly tries to understand his position, believing that the matter can be resolved to their mutual satisfaction. If you find yourself in that position, assure others that you want to find an acceptable solution. Ask if they have suggestions. Once the situation is resolved, follow up with friendly words and chats.

Teaching the Win/Win Resolution Process to Students

If you teach the win/win resolution process to your students and help them practice it, you can remove yourself from the role of perpetual arbitrator and fix-it person. At a class meeting, bring up the topic of conflicts. Mention examples that might arise in class or on the grounds. Ask students about the damaging results of resolutions that produce a winner and a loser. Introduce the win/win strategy. Provide opportunities for students to practice it. Show them how to use the following tactics if confronted with a potentially serious dispute (Nelsen, Lott, and Glenn, 2000):

1. Ignore the situation.
2. Talk the situation over respectfully with the other student.
3. Find a win/win solution.
4. If no solution can be found, put the item on the class meeting agenda for the class to discuss.

In the room display a chart listing the four tactics. When students get involved in arguments, point to the chart and ask them if they have tried any of the tactics. If they haven't, ask them which they would like to try. This takes you out of the middle and helps students learn to resolve conflicts on their own.

QUESTIONS FOR SELF-IMPROVEMENT

1. What is your understanding of "congruent communication?" Can you give three examples?

2. The listed "roadblocks" to communication are things almost all teachers do. Are they so bad? Why do you think Gordon is so opposed to them?

3. Sarcasm was depicted as something never to be used in class, yet many very witty people use it as stock in trade. Where do you draw the line between sarcasm that is funny and sarcasm that is hurtful?

ACTIVITIES FOR SELF-IMPROVEMENT

1. Analyze yourself concerning your use of congruent communication. How do you feel you rate, overall? Write out five statements to use when responding to student misbehavior that you feel would maintain good relations.

2. Respond to either (a) or (b):

   a. If you are naturally at ease with strangers and able to communicate with no difficulty, write out how you do so, as a guide for others to follow.

   b. If you are ill at ease with strangers and have difficulty communicating with them, write out a plan for what you can do and say to counter the awkwardness you normally experience.

3. Suppose you want to apply the "builders" Nelsen, Lott, and Glenn advocate in place of the corresponding "barriers." Select a lesson of your choice and indicate how, in its presentation, you would use builders while avoiding barriers.

4. Compose four conflict scenarios to use in teaching students to use win/win conflict resolution.

15 Implementing Helpful Discipline in Your Class

This chapter describes a procedure for introducing Helpful Discipline and implementing it in the classroom. Directions are given for conducting seven protocol sessions that draw students into meaningful collaboration and establish class agreements.

The Class Meeting Format

Class discussions, such as those described in this chapter, should be conducted using the class meeting format. You may have to teach students how class meetings are conducted. Ask them to sit in a close circle so that each person can see all others. Begin the discussion by introducing a concern or need. For example, tell students you'd like their input on how they'd like the class to function. Point out that, in order for their contributions to be made effectively, the discussions must follow certain rules:

- Everyone gets equal opportunity to speak.
- Each person is entitled to express his or her opinion and be heard by all.
- No one is to interrupt or make fun of others.
- All suggestions are considered.
- No one is allowed to dominate the discussion.

Write these rules on a chart that can be displayed for easy reference and referred to when necessary.

Purposes and Procedures of the Introductory Sessions

The purposes of the introductory sessions are to

1. establish a collaborative relationship with your students;
2. engage students in dialog concerning how the class might best serve everyone's needs;

3. reach class agreements about matters such as curriculum, instruction, class character, behavior, discipline, interpersonal relations, and quality.

As the discussions proceed, you may wish to consider additional topics.

In the discussions, there is no need for you to mention Helpful Discipline by name. Don't say, "Here is a great plan for us to follow . . . It is great because . . . And here's what we need to do . . . " Instead, ask questions that make students think about behavior and procedures in the class, and in that manner allow them to form conclusions about what will serve them well and what will not. Their conclusions should be formalized as succinct statements, thereafter called "class agreements." The value of those agreements depends in part on students' willingness to support them. Such willingness is normally strong provided students have helped formulate the agreements and grasp how they serve individual and collective interests. One of the agreements should describe what is to be done, helpfully and positively, when a student or teacher violates a class agreement.

The program can be introduced in a series of approximately seven sessions. From fourth grade through senior high school, each of the sessions requires about twenty minutes or, in some cases, a bit more. In primary grades, the sessions can be completed in ten to fifteen minutes. The following illustrations are generic, for the middle school level. Modify them as necessary to make them appropriate for your students and situation.

It was mentioned that, for these discussions, students should be seated in a tight circle. If your classroom, lab, shop, or gymnasium does not allow this possibility, make the best arrangement you can so that students have eye contact with each other.

Session #1. Presenting Yourself to Students, and Students to You

This session presumes that you and the class are new to each other. If you decide to introduce Helpful Discipline after you have already been working with a class and know the members, skip this session.

As students come into the class area, smile at them, make eye contact, and greet them verbally. When you have helped them settle into a circle, tell them you are pleased to see them, eager to know them better, and are looking forward to working with them. Say you are excited about the class and want to get their ideas on how to make it as useful and enjoyable as possible. From the class list, call each student by name. Make eye contact, smile, and, if necessary, ask if you have pronounced the name correctly. Do your best to learn all names as quickly as possible—this is very important to students. Do this expeditiously; don't draw it out.

In no more than two minutes, tell students just a bit about yourself. Let your personality show while maintaining your decorum. Very briefly mention your family, pets, hobbies, and interests, but keep this short. (In future days and weeks you can add more details about yourself, such as places you have traveled, special skills you possess, and unusual experiences you've had. Explain why you became a teacher and what you have liked most about it.)

After introducing yourself, tell the students you'd like to learn something about them. From your class roster, call on individual students or ask them to work in pairs and introduce each other. Suggest they mention something especially memorable about themselves, such as unusual hobbies or experiences. Move quickly and try to get around to all students, even if it makes the meeting run long. As the session ends, thank the students and tell them that at the next session you want to learn what they like and dislike about school.

Session #2. Drawing Students Out on How They'd Like the Class to Function

Have with you a chart and marker so you can take notes. Tell the students you are interested in organizing the class (or improving its organization) so it helps them learn important information and allows them to have an enjoyable time. Begin by asking:

1. What are some of the things you like best about school?

   (They will probably say they like sports, being with friends, playing, doing art and music. Some may mention performing in plays, concerts, and athletics. A few may mention learning, good teachers, computers, laboratories, and library.)

   Down the left side of your chart make a list of what they say.

2. Ask what they like, specifically, about each of the things you've listed. Write their comments on the right side of your chart.

3. Ask if they think it would be possible for this class to have some of the things they've mentioned. Circle the ones they think possible.

Thank the students for their contributions. Tell them you want the class to include topics and activities they enjoy insofar as possible. Tell them you will follow up on their suggestions at the next discussion.

Session #3. Feedback on Previous Suggestion, and Drawing Students Out on What They Prefer in Teachers

Begin the session by reiterating what students previously said they like best in school. Ask if you have understood their comments correctly. Reassure them that you will give their suggestions serious consideration. Turn to a fresh page on the chart and

1. Ask if they have had a teacher they really enjoyed and respected. Ask them not to mention names, but indicate what that teacher did that made such a good impression. (They will probably say the teacher was nice, neat, interest-

ing, helpful, fair, and had a sense of humor. They may mention activities they liked or the teacher's special talents.) Write what students say down the left side of your chart.

2. Review students' comments. Where needed, ask for elaboration, such as, What does a "nice" (or "neat") teacher do? What does a helpful teacher do? What does "we really had fun" mean? Make notes on the right side of the chart.

3. Tell students you want to be the kind of teacher they prefer, insofar as you can. Tell them you will give feedback on their suggestions at the next discussion and see how you can incorporate them into your style of teaching. Thank them for their thoughtfulness.

Session #4. Feedback on Preferred Teacher Traits, and Drawing Students Out Concerning Behavior in Class

Review students' comments about teachers from the previous session. Ask if they have corrections or additions. Reassure them that you will try to be the sort of teacher they enjoy insofar as you can.

Now draw students out concerning how they like their classmates to behave in school.

1. Ask students to think of a classmate who has behaved in ways they admired or appreciated. Without naming names, let them describe the classmate. List the behaviors down the left side of your chart.

2. When several behaviors are listed, go back and ask why those behaviors are appreciated. List the comments on the right side of the chart.

3. Ask students how they like fellow members of classes to treat them. Make notes on the left side and go back and again ask why.

4. Expand the question to the kinds of behavior they most appreciate from other students when the teacher is presenting a lesson or they are working together on assignments. Ask why. Just before the end of the session, ask students if they agree on the behaviors and reasons you have listed on your chart. Ask if they think it would be possible to have those kinds of behavior in this classroom.

Thank them for their input. Tell them you will keep the notes for further consideration.

Session #5. Feedback on Desirable Behavior, and Exploration of Undesirable Behavior

Quickly review students' contributions about behavior they appreciate in others in various situations. Verify that you have summarized their ideas correctly.

Now ask about the kind of behavior they *dislike* in their classmates. On the left of your chart, make a list of the disliked behaviors. Ask students why they dislike them. Jot the reasons on the right side of the page.

When several behaviors have been listed, ask students why those behaviors occur. Then ask how they might be prevented from occurring. Your students may have some trouble with this, so ask if there are things teachers and students can do that will cause students to *want* to behave properly, not things that make them afraid to misbehave. Take notes. If they get stuck, ask directly about removing causes of misbehavior, providing enjoyable activities, and living by the Golden Rule.

After they have shared some ideas, say something like the following: "Suppose despite everything we do, someone in the class misbehaves, does something that we as a class do not approve of. What should we do then?" Students typically suggest punishment of some sort; therefore ask, "Could we help those persons understand their behavior is harmful to the class or to themselves? Does punishing help them, or does it just make them feel bad?" Tell students you don't want to use punishment or be unpleasant or fight against them in any way. "That doesn't do us any good. What I'd prefer is to correct whatever is causing the person to misbehave. That is how I would like to go about it. Put yourself in that student's place. Would you prefer being punished or having conditions changed so you simply wouldn't feel like misbehaving any more?"

Thank the students for taking the matter seriously. Tell them that, in the next session, you will explore how their suggestions might be put into practice.

Session #6. Preparing Class Agreements

Before the session, prepare a fresh chart that summarizes the following:

> What students said they like best about school.
> What students said they like best in teachers.
> Behavior students said they like in classmates.
> Behavior students said they dislike in classmates.
> How class members who misbehave might be helped to behave better.

Show students the chart and say: "Here are the ideas you have had about what makes school enjoyable and worthwhile. I'd like to see if you would be willing to add a sixth item that says all of us, you and I, will make a strong effort to do high quality work. Would you agree to that?" (Explain what you mean by "high quality" and discuss the point as necessary.)

Say: "Now I'm wondering how we might make these things happen in our class. You have said you like school to be interesting and fun, and in that regard you have mentioned studying interesting topics, working together with friends, and having more group activity and less working by yourself. If you want to agree to that, let's make a statement about it and together we will do our best to make everything we do as enjoyable as possible." The class might come up with the following statement: "We agree to do our best to make school interesting and enjoyable." Follow with the remaining topics, and make a class agreement about each of them. You may need an extra session for this. When this activity is completed, prepare a chart that shows the agreements and display it in class. Give it a prominent title, such as "Our Class Agreements."

Suppose your class has settled on the following agreements (given for illustration only):

1. We will do our best to make the class interesting and enjoyable.
2. Our personal behavior will always be ethical, considerate, and responsible.
3. We will keep the classroom orderly and comfortable.
4. We will do high quality work we can be proud of.
5. If anyone breaks an agreement, we will do what we can to help the person want to behave properly.

Session #7. Intervening Helpfully When Misbehavior Occurs

Display a chart of the agreements in the class. Say: "Here are the agreements we reached previously that will guide our behavior in the class. Look at them again. Are there any you want to change? delete? add?"

"All right, then. Let's suppose somebody breaks one of the agreements. We have said that, if that happens, we will help the individual conduct him- or herself properly once again. I'd like to suggest that it will be my duty to intervene—that is, to step in and take action—when agreements are broken. You can assist by being considerate toward the person we are trying to help. When I intervene, here is what I'll attempt to accomplish:

- stop the misbehavior;
- remove the cause of misbehavior, if I can determine what it is;
- help the person return to proper behavior;
- reduce the likelihood that the situation will occur again;
- leave the person's feelings and dignity intact.

If the misbehavior is relatively serious, I may want to discuss it with the entire class. Sometimes this is desirable, sometimes not. I'll use my judgment about that. If misbehavior is very serious, I may need to call the office for immediate assistance.

"Now, what do you think I should do or say when someone is misbehaving and I need to intervene?" Jot the class's suggestions on a chart. After some discussion, the class might arrive at suggestions such as the following. If they are agreeable to you, write them out. Make sure the class understands that you may use any of them, in any order. Explain that you will point to or otherwise indicate the agreement being violated and do or say:

For minor misbehavior
- Nothing more than make eye contact with the student.
- "Perhaps I can remind you of this agreement?"
- "I am not comfortable with what is happening here. Could I ask for your consideration and help?"

For lethargy or lack of interest
- "I can tell you are not very interested in this (topic or activity). What can I do to make the experience better for you?" (Suggestions are considered at this time.)
- "Class, this doesn't seem to be working as we had hoped. What do you think the problem is? Can we resolve it, or should we change to a different activity?" (Suggestions are considered at this time.)
- "Class, I don't feel (something such as the quality of our work recently) has been up to the expectations we hold for ourselves. Perhaps we might discuss this matter in a class meeting." (The class meeting is held later, involving problem solving.)

For recurring difficulties
- "We are having problems keeping this agreement. Why is that, and how can we resolve the matter?" (Suggestions are considered at this point. Problem solving is used.)

For resistant problems or conflicts
- "Could you meet with me later? We need to work together to straighten this out." (Public discussion or private conference follows. Problem solving is used for resolution.)

For hurtful events or serious conflicts
- "Let's meet together and see if we can help each other work this out." (Conference ensues. Plans are made for resolution and follow-up.)
- "When you have cooled down, let's talk together to see if we can settle this problem." (Private conference follows. Conflict resolution is used.)

For gross defiance or dangerous behavior
- "You must go immediately to (separate parts of the room; suspension room; principal's office). I really hope we can talk about this later and get it settled."
- Call office for immediate assistance, if necessary.

Refining the Agreements over Time

Once class agreements have been formalized and put in place, review them periodically with the class. Ask if they are clear, if they are serving well, and if they need to be modified in any way. You may wish to devote one or more class meetings to considering all the agreements, making sure students understand them fully. Ask for examples and explanations. Agreement #1, for example, was "We will do our best to make the class interesting and enjoyable." Discussion about this agreement might be guided by questions such as:

Who decides if something is worth learning about? How is the decision made? What if there is disagreement about its importance? What determines whether instructional activities are enjoyable? Who decides? What if there is disagreement about enjoyment?

Discussion of agreement #2 ("Our personal behavior will always be ethical, considerate, and responsible") might be guided by questions such as:

Why would we want to treat others as was done? How do we want others to treat us? How do we not want to be treated? What can we do when we are not being treated well?

The remaining agreements are clarified in the same manner.

Enhancing Program Effectiveness

You can expect students to support Helpful Discipline and collaborate with you to make it successful. As the program gets under way, you should see an immediate reduction in misbehavior with a corresponding increase in enthusiasm and satisfaction. The program won't remove all misbehavior, but it will encourage positive relationships and allow learning to occur with relatively few disruptions.

Meanwhile, you continually enhance your program by modeling, teaching, and/or discussing matters such as causes of misbehavior, dealing with those causes, meeting everyone's needs, considering others, developing character, communicating considerately, improving personal relations, working together collaboratively, enjoying school to the fullest, and growing in self-control and responsibility. Consider making such instruction and discussion a regular part of your curriculum.

You will soon be very pleased with how well-behaved your students become and how much they learn. They will interact in a friendly, considerate manner. They will show a positive attitude toward school, the class, and you. They will enjoy the instructional activities in which they engage. They will work agreeably and helpfully with you and each other. They will increasingly show initiative, self-direction, and responsibility and will make a strong effort to do quality work.

All this is accomplished without your having to cajole or reprimand. Students will embrace the partnership with you and enjoy working together to ensure quality education. They will very much appreciate the confidence you show in them and your continual willingness to help.

QUESTIONS FOR SELF-IMPROVEMENT

1. To what extent are you comfortable with allowing students the quantity of input suggested in this chapter? Explain.

2. Some people contend that lead-teaching requires more effort than boss-teaching, and does not necessarily produce better results. Do you agree or disagree? Is your answer the same for all topics in the curriculum?

3. Why go to all the trouble of drawing out students' feelings and opinions when you already know, for the most part, what they are going to say?

ACTIVITIES FOR SELF-IMPROVEMENT

1. Select one of the example class agreements shown at the end of Session #6 and describe how you would help the class clarify it further.

2. Examine Sessions #2 and #3. Reword them to make them suitable for a class at a higher or lower grade level.

3. Describe how you would intervene if

    a. a student withdraws completely from the lesson;

    b. a student swears at another, or at you;

    c. a student, or the class, turns in work of quality that is far below expectations;

    d. the class moans when you introduce the next assignment;

    e. the class is so noisy or so messy it is driving you nuts.

CHAPTER 16

In Review: The Nature and Procedures of Helpful Discipline

The Discipline Problem

Poor discipline, meaning chronic student misbehavior, is severely damaging education everywhere. It is harming student learning, frustrating teachers, and shortchanging parents, society, and taxpayers. Although nobody wants poor discipline, it remains entrenched and is, by most accounts, growing worse.

We now have the means for reversing that trend. The solution lies in working with students in a way that avoids force, intimidation, belittlement, threat, or punishment. The predominant—and essential—quality of this more effective approach is helpfulness. The approach never tries to "make" students do anything, yet it enables students to relinquish self-defeating behavior, enjoy positive relationships with teachers and fellow students, acquire a strong sense of personal dignity, control themselves, resolve conflicts productively, and strengthen personal character along with that of the class as a whole. The approach is called Helpful Discipline.

Helpful Discipline

Helpful Discipline is the most powerful approach we have for maintaining truly effective discipline. It places high emphasis on ethics, trust, and joy. It is aligned with students' needs and the goals of education, which it always complements and never contravenes. It also gives attention to teacher needs, recognizing that teachers cannot effectively use discipline tactics that are contrary to their personal needs.

Helpful Discipline is collaborative, with teacher and students working together closely to plan and conduct the class. It anticipates difficulties and prepares for them in advance. It promotes self-control and teaches students to behave responsibly. It builds strong student character and promotes quality communication and human relations.

Educators who wish to implement Helpful Discipline must complete several specific tasks:

Replace inaccurate concepts of discipline with correct ones.
Understand basic human needs that require attention in education.

Make curriculum and instruction compatible with educational needs and goals. Identify types and causes of misbehavior and learn how they are addressed.

Understand how to work helpfully with students instead of coercing them.

Understand the value and procedures of teacher–student collaboration.

Learn how to prevent misbehavior and support student self-control.

Learn how to intervene helpfully and productively when misbehavior occurs. Understand the meaning, importance, and development of class character.

Examine techniques and effects of communication and human relations.

Learn how to introduce and implement Helpful Discipline.

Establishing Correct Concepts of Discipline

Your first task in preparing for Helpful Discipline is to eliminate faulty concepts of discipline and replace them with accurate ones, as follows:

*Eliminate: "The discipline problem is too complex to do anything about."

Replace with: *Misbehavior is caused by specific, identifiable reasons we can do something about.*

*Eliminate: "When students misbehave, it is because they choose to do so."

Replace with: *Misbehavior tends to occur naturally, in accordance with existing conditions.*

*Eliminate: "Misbehavior is the fault of students, parents, teachers, or society."

Replace with: *Misbehavior occurs for specific reasons we can identify and correct.*

*Eliminate: "Discipline is what teachers do to stifle misbehavior when it occurs."

Replace with: *Discipline is a broad strategy designed to help students profit best from the school experience.*

*Eliminate: "Effective discipline must involve force, coercion, and threat."

Replace with: *Force, coercion, and threat are detrimental to effective discipline and should be replaced with consideration, kindness, and helpfulness.*

*Eliminate: "Teachers automatically know how to relate productively with students."

Replace with: *We can improve the ways we relate to and work with students.*

*Eliminate: "The established curriculum should not be altered."

Replace with: *Reasonable changes in the curriculum can help students learn better, enjoy the process, and maintain desirable attitudes.*

Basic Human Needs

Your second task in preparing for Helpful Discipline is to familiarize yourself with seven basic human needs that affect behavior in the classroom: security, belonging, hope, dignity, power, enjoyment, and competence. You must recognize how the needs affect, and are made evident in, student behavior, how you identify them, how you attend to them when necessary, and how you organize your educational program to make it consistent with those needs.

Each of the seven basic needs is accompanied by a number of "surface needs" that become evident when a given basic need requires attention. By satisfying those surface needs you simultaneously satisfy the underlying basic need.

Your Basic Needs

Your third task in preparing for Helpful Discipline is to make sure your own needs are met in the classroom. The seven basic needs that apply to students apply to you as well—the needs for security, belonging, hope, dignity, power, enjoyment, and competence. When any of your needs is not being met at school, you become less confident and more erratic, and your pleasure and satisfaction decline.

As do students, you will experience a number of different "surface needs and behaviors" when any of your basic needs is going unmet. Those surface behaviors indicate the unmet need and provide guidance for satisfying it. Make it a priority to satisfy your needs along with those of your students.

Satisfaction and Enjoyment

Your fourth task in preparing for Helpful Discipline is to learn how to make your curriculum satisfying and your instruction enjoyable for students. When you manage that, students learn more, behave better, and maintain better attitudes.

You accomplish this by making sure your teaching and discipline programs are fully compatible with student needs, your needs, and the goals of education. The goals of education are your starting point, indicating what you intend to achieve. Most educators agree that the goals include quality academic learning, good citizenship, a positive attitude toward learning, an ability to relate well with others, and positive self-control and self-direction. Use those goals to make sure everything you do in class contributes to the results you want.

Align your curriculum—the program of topics you want students to study—with the goals of education. Do the same with your instructional activities. Make sure that the curriculum and instruction are also compatible with students' needs. This may require adjustments in the established curriculum. You are allowed and expected to make these adjustments, within reason, of course. Make your class activities interesting and fun. Consider working as a "lead teacher" who entices and energizes students rather than as a "boss teacher" who tells students what to do and directs everything. Remember that students will engage willingly in activities that allow them to talk, work in groups, move about, do creative activities, and collaborate on projects. They very much appreciate variety, novelty, challenge, mystery, repetition, music, active movement, telling stories, role playing, and using computers. Don't forget—your need for enjoyable activities is important, too.

Presenting Yourself Attractively

Your fifth task in preparing for Helpful Discipline is to learn to present yourself attractively to students, who react strongly to the impressions you make as a teacher and person. You make the best impression by being charismatic and showing you are ethical, helpful, and considerate. You show your ethical qualities by always being honest and fair and never intentionally harming your students.

You must not speak to anyone at school disdainfully or hurtfully, even when they show disrespect for you. When students see your exemplary behavior, they begin to trust you. Helpfulness is very attractive, too; it shows you want students to succeed. Continually ask yourself, "Is what I am doing right now helpful to my students?" or "What could I do right now that would be most helpful?"

You show consideration by being aware of your students' characteristics, needs, feelings, and the circumstances influencing them at a given time. Behave toward your students in accordance with that awareness. Make sure you don't give offense when expressing opinions, giving directions, and providing feedback.

Strive to project a degree of charisma. Students are drawn to it and it makes them more inclined to listen and cooperate with you. You can increase charisma by talking with students in an engaging way, sharing special talents, knowledge, and skills, and giving them glimpses of your personal life. Smile at your students, be friendly, share your knowledge, show your enthusiasm, yet always be sensitive and compassionate.

Present yourself as an effective leader, too. Raise issues, establish the direction and agenda, set the tone, make it easy for students to do their work, provide help, and assume ultimate responsibility. In the process, consult with, secure the collaboration of, and delegate responsibility to your students.

Collaborating with Students

Your sixth task in preparing for Helpful Discipline is to learn how to bring your students into close collaboration in resolving class problems and making decisions about behavior and the class program. Collaboration produces a number of benefits. It puts you and your students on the same side, working together to ensure effective teaching, learning, and class behavior. It gives students a much-needed sense of positive power and inclines them to abide by decisions they help make. It establishes students' stake in maintaining the well-being of the class and does away with the somewhat antagonistic posture often seen between teacher and students. And it makes possible some of the most important functions of Helpful Discipline, such as meeting needs, providing mutual support, developing self-direction and self-control, establishing trust and consideration for others, and establishing a class sense of community.

The more closely you collaborate with students, the more purposeful and responsible they become. Without collaboration, you are likely to find yourself frequently at odds with students, with none of you fully able to meet your needs or enjoy the class.

Once the collaborative process becomes operational, the class (and you) will experience a growing sense of belonging and community. Help students gain confidence that they can succeed and contribute. Involve them meaningfully in decision making. Remove the fear of making mistakes. Make sure students see evidence that collaboration is working and they are making progress.

Understanding Misbehavior

Your seventh task in preparing for Helpful Discipline is to understand the meaning of misbehavior, the types of misbehavior normally encountered, and the causes of misbehavior. In Helpful Discipline, classroom misbehavior is defined as any behavior that, through *intent* or *thoughtlessness*, interferes with teaching or learning, threatens or intimidates others, or oversteps society's standards of moral, ethical, or legal behavior.

In most cases misbehavior occurs naturally from the interplay between student nature and the conditions being experienced at a given time, such as excitement, threat, provocation, fear, boredom, hopelessness, frustration, or isolation.

You should, therefore, organize class conditions that prompt students to behave properly, in a natural manner. This means giving up forcefulness and authoritarianism in favor of considerate helpfulness, aligning your program with student needs, making your program highly interesting, presenting yourself engagingly, and drawing students into collaborative cooperation. You can further improve behavior by identifying and discussing with students the types of misbehavior and the factors known to cause them.

Addressing the Causes of Misbehavior
that Originate in Students

Your eighth task in preparing for Helpful Discipline is to learn how to remove, deactivate, or ameliorate causes of behavior that originate in individuals and groups of students. By successfully deactivating causes, you prevent or correct corresponding misbehavior.

You can address *expediency* through discussing its troublesome effects and helping students see that it often works against their best interests.

You counter students' *urge to transgress* by behaving in an exemplary manner and discussing the harm that occurs when class agreements are broken, not only to individuals who transgress but to others who are affected.

You counter *temptation* through frank discussions that analyze temptation and foresee its potentially dangerous consequences.

You address *inappropriate habits* through discussions that make students aware of them and their undesirable effects. You can also directly teach students how to behave acceptably and provide opportunity for them to do so.

You address *poor behavior choices* through discussions about surface needs and how to attend to them in a positive manner.

You address *avoidance* through discussions about what students try to avoid in school, why they do so, what can be properly avoided and what cannot, and how students can deal effectively with what they cannot avoid.

You address *egocentric personalities* through discussions about whether the needs and interests of all students are important or whether only certain students deserve attention, whether or not everyone is entitled to equal opportunity in the class, and what can be done to ensure equal opportunities for everyone.

You address *provocation* through discussions about whether provoking others is useful in the classroom, and if it is not, why it occurs and how it can be kept to a minimum.

You address *group behavior* through discussions about how and why students behave differently in groups than individually, how to distinguish between the helpful and harmful effects of peer pressure and group spirit, and how the harmful effects can be avoided.

Addressing the Causes of Misbehavior Caused by Learning Environments and Adult Personnel

Your ninth task in preparing for Helpful Discipline is to learn to address causes of misbehavior that originate in instructional environments and adult school personnel.

You correct *physical discomfort* by making sure lighting, temperature, seating, and work spaces are comfortable.

You address *tedium* by breaking work into shorter segments and increasing the interest level.

You address *meaninglessness* by making sure students see the relevance, importance, and applicability of topics to their lives.

You correct *lack of motivation* by providing study topics that have natural appeal or by exploring them through activities students especially enjoy.

You address *poor models of behavior* by always behaving in an exemplary manner when with students.

You address *showing little interest in or appreciation for students* by giving each student as much personal attention as possible, through smiles, help, friendly chats, consideration, making them comfortable, and acknowledging their progress.

You address *disregarding students' feelings* by keeping yourself attuned to their feelings, not only of happiness and optimism, but also of distress, sadness, frustration, fear, boredom, and pessimism. Acknowledge their feelings considerately. Talk about them when appropriate. Show you are sympathetic with the emotions they are experiencing and are ready to help however you can.

You address *uninteresting lessons* by avoiding the dull lesson trap, making sure your lessons are attractive and that you display genuine enthusiasm.

You address problems of *ineffective guidance and feedback* by making sure students understand clearly what they are supposed to do, how to do it, and how they can improve.

You address *communicating ineffectively* by sharing pleasantries with students, exchanging views with them, and letting them know what is expected of them in class.

You address *coercion, threat, and punishment* by replacing them with kindness, considerate helpfulness, personal attention, and good communication. You cannot force students to learn or behave properly; you only harm them, and yourself, when you try to do so.

Preventing Misbehavior, Supporting Proper Behavior, and Correcting Misbehavior

Your tenth task in preparing for Helpful Discipline is to learn to prevent misbehavior, support student self-control, and correct misbehavior when it occurs. These aspects of discipline are sometimes called "preventive discipline," "supportive discipline," and "corrective discipline."

Preventive discipline brings great payoff for relatively little effort. You prevent misbehavior by being friendly, helpful, and courteous to your students, aligning your program with human needs, and making curriculum and instruction as enjoyable as possible. You collaborate with students in reaching agreements about class behavior and procedures. You provide the best model of ethical behavior possible. You discuss misbehavior, its effects, its causes, and how it can be avoided, and you plan proactively to foresee and avoid potential problems.

Supportive discipline is applied when students are beginning to lose self-control and are on the verge of misbehaving. Tactics helpful in supportive discipline include injecting enthusiasm, catching students' eyes, moving alongside edgy students, showing interest in their work, asking them cheerful questions or making favorable comments, providing a light challenge, and talking personally and helpfully with students inclined to misbehave.

Corrective discipline is applied when you stop misbehavior, get the student back on track, and preserve positive feelings and relations. The best way to do this is by following the class agreements you and your students have established collaboratively. Those agreements identify approved behavior and specify how misbehavior should be addressed.

When you intervene, be helpful and reasonable, not forceful or punitive. Make sure you give no personal offense to students, and strive to maintain good relationships. Good interventions often involve follow-through. It is important that offending students acknowledge their misbehavior. Give them ownership of the problem and responsibility for correcting it. This might involve making restitution, dealing with what caused the misbehavior, making amends, and practicing suitable alternative behaviors.

Occasionally you will make mistakes when dealing with misbehavior. You may "misbehave" by treating students improperly or violating class agreements. When you do so, apologize sincerely and ask students to help you avoid repeating the mistake in the future.

Improving Class Character

Your eleventh task in preparing for Helpful Discipline is to learn how to improve the overall character, or personality, of your class. Class character is comprised of thirteen qualities, all of which can be easily assessed and improved.

Ethics: Class members treat each other kindly, honestly, and fairly. Ethical qualities grow as you provide a good model and encourage class members to treat each other well and do the right thing.

Trust: Class members are comfortable with the teacher and each other, confident of being treated in a kind and helpful manner. Trust develops as you and your students adhere to ethical principles and show genuine concern for each other.

Consideration: Class members are sensitive to each other's feelings, comfort, and dignity. Consideration grows as class members recognize and show tolerance for each other's traits, beliefs, attitudes, values, and needs.

Dignity: Class members are considerate of each other and treat each other with courtesy and respect. Dignity grows stronger as we acknowledge each other's competencies and feel valued and respected by others.

Personal power: Class members make decisions, direct themselves, and accept responsibility for their actions. Personal power grows stronger when you help students make decisions and assume control of various aspects of their lives.

Opportunity: Class members have abundant opportunity to participate, learn, and use instructional materials. Opportunity is strengthened when you make sure students always have access to a variety of learning possibilities and necessary materials.

Purposefulness: Class members have clear notions of what they are to accomplish, why it is important, and how they are to proceed. Purposefulness grows stronger as students identify and pursue topics they truly want to learn about, plan what they hope to accomplish, indicate how they will go about it, identify needed resources and where to get them, and determine what evidence will tell them they have accomplished their intentions.

Persistence: Class members work diligently, do not give up easily, and strive for quality. Persistence grows as you encourage students to stick with tasks and follow them through to completion, even when the tasks are difficult and frustrating.

Responsibility: Class members pursue tasks, complete them satisfactorily in accordance with existing conditions, accept credit or blame for the results, and make corrections or recompense when necessary. Responsibility is strengthened when you provide frequent opportunities for students to undertake important tasks, make decisions about procedures and self-conduct, complete the tasks satisfactorily given the conditions, and show how they have achieved the results.

Energy: Class members show a high level of purposeful activity when it is appropriate to do so. Energy is increased when you provide an interesting curriculum, enjoyable activities, personal interaction, charisma, and a strong sense of purpose.

Helpfulness: Class members routinely offer to help others in need. Helpfulness is strengthened as you show continual willingness to help and encourage all members of the class to help each other.

Collaboration: Teacher and students work together to attain the goals of education in a manner each considers productive and enjoyable. Collaboration grows as you draw students into genuine partnership with you to make all aspects of class life as enjoyable and satisfying as possible.

Joy: Sense of pleasure and satisfaction pervades the class. Joy is strengthened when students pursue topics they find fascinating, participate in enjoyable activities, and associate with teachers and fellow students who are trustworthy and engaging.

Improving Communication and Human Relations

The twelfth task you must complete in preparing for Helpful Discipline involves improving communication and human relations in your classes. *Communication*, as the term is used here, refers to the effects people's comments have on others. Human relations refer to how individuals treat each other.

Good class communication helps students get along better and cooperate more willingly. It is improved through congruent communication, avoiding communication roadblocks, and using builders rather than barriers.

Congruent communication involves saying things that are harmonious with students' feelings about situations and themselves. It addresses undesirable behavior without embarrassing students or putting them on the defensive. It does not preach, moralize, impose guilt, or demand promises, but, instead, confers dignity on students.

Communication roadblocks often occur when you try to help students who are experiencing difficulty, but in doing so you push them away from you and they become disinclined to communicate. Examples of such roadblocks are giving orders, issuing warnings, preaching, advising, criticizing, and questioning. These tactics usually make students feel worse and less inclined to work productively. You should replace roadblocks with offers of helpfulness.

Teachers unknowingly do and say things that can affect students positively or negatively. Statements that are respectful and encouraging are called "builders," while statements that are disrespectful and discouraging are called "barriers." An example of a barrier is saying, "You knew what I wanted on this assignment." A builder would be, "What was your understanding of the assignment?"

Human relations have to do with the ways we treat each other in various situations. We hope to make a good impression, open up communication, confer dignity, use positive body language, and react positively to others. We hope *not* to slight other people, put them down, or speak sarcastically.

It is important to teach students how to deal with problems and conflicts. Problems are difficulties needing resolution so that everyone agrees. Conflicts are issues that pit one person against another and involve strong emotions. Problems can be solved using the standard problem-solving procedure. Conflicts should be resolved on a win/win basis that allows all disputants to get most of what they want.

Introducing and Implementing Helpful Discipline in the Classroom

Helpful Discipline is best introduced and implemented through a series of class discussions, rather than being handed to students as a prescription for class behavior. The discussions employ a class meeting format and are used to establish a collaborative relationship with students, explore how the class might best serve everyone's needs, and formulate class agreements concerning behavior and the class program. The suggested sequence of introductory discussions is as follows:

1. *Presenting yourself to students, and students to you.* Make eye contact with all students, greet them, learn their names, learn a bit about each of them, and tell a bit about yourself.

2. *Drawing students out on how they'd like the class to function.* Ask students what they like best in school and if they think it is possible to have some of those things in this class. Take notes.

3. *Drawing students out on what they prefer in teachers.* Ask students what they have enjoyed most in their favorite teachers. Explore what they mean if the descriptive words are not clear. Tell them which of their preferences you think you can provide in the class.

4. *Drawing students out on class behavior they prefer.* Ask students how they like fellow class members to treat them. Ask how they feel they should conduct themselves. List the desirable behaviors and ask students if they think such behavior is possible in this class.

5. *Explore undesirable behavior.* Ask students about the kinds of behavior they dislike in a class or in their classmates. Ask why they dislike those behaviors. Ask how this class might prevent them.

6. *Reach class agreements about behavior, teaching, and the class program.* Ask class members to compose agreements about life in the class. When five or six statements are finalized, ask how the class can make these desirable things happen almost all the time.

7. *Reach an agreement about how you should intervene when students violate class agreements.* Explore how you can stop the misbehavior, help the offender to behave better in the future, and maintain good feelings. Post the agreement in the room and follow it when you must intervene in misbehavior.

Review of Tasks in Preparing for Helpful Discipline

1. Make sure you have accurate, productive concepts of class discipline.
2. Recognize basic human needs that affect discipline.
3. Recognize your personal needs and how they affect discipline.
4. Increase student satisfaction and enjoyment by aligning your program with goals and needs.
5. Learn how to present yourself engagingly to students.
6. Learn how to bring students into collaboration with you.
7. Understand the meaning and types of misbehavior.
8. Learn to address causes of misbehavior that originate in students.
9. Learn to address causes of misbehavior that originate in school environments and personnel.
10. Learn the nature and requirements of preventive, supportive, and corrective discipline.
11. Understand class character, its components, how it affects discipline, and how it is strengthened.
12. Learn how to improve communication and human relations in the classroom.

S E L F - T E S T   O N   H E L P F U L   D I S C I P L I N E

Can you answer the following questions related to Helpful Discipline?

1. What is "the discipline problem?"

2. Why is it so serious?

3. How can it be resolved?

4. Why do human needs require attention in discipline?

5. How can you attend to the basic needs important in discipline?

6. How can you align curriculum and instruction with human needs and goals of education?

7. How can you present yourself engagingly to students?

8. Why is collaborating with your students so important?

9. How can you draw your students into genuine collaboration with you?

10. What is misbehavior, and what types of misbehavior are seen in most classrooms?

11. What causes misbehavior?

12. How can you remove or lessen the causes of misbehavior?

13. How can you prevent student misbehavior?

14. How can you support student self-control?

15. How should you intervene when students misbehave?

16. What is meant by "class character," and what are its components?

17. How does "class character" affect discipline?

18. How can you strengthen class character?

19. How does communication affect discipline?

20. How can you improve communication in your class?

21. How do human relations affect discipline?

22. How can you strengthen human relations in your classes?

23. What are conflicts, and how are they best resolved?

24. What is the nature of Helpful Discipline?

25. How do you introduce and implement Helpful Discipline in your class?

REFERENCES

Albert, L. 1996. *Cooperative discipline.* Circle Pines, MN: American Guidance Service.

Canter, L. 1992. *Assertive discipline: A take-charge approach for today's educator.* Seal Beach, CA: Canter & Associates.

Charles, C. 2000. *The synergetic classroom: Joyful teaching and gentle discipline.* New York: Longman.

Chiu, L., & Tulley, M. 1997. Student preferences of teacher discipline styles. *Journal of Instructional Psychology, 24*(3), 168–176.

Coloroso, B. 1994. *Kids are worth it!: Giving your child the gift of inner discipline.* New York: Avon.

———. 1999. *Parenting with wit and wisdom in times of chaos and confusion.* Littleton, CO: Kids are worth it!

Covey, S. 1989. *The seven habits of highly effective people.* New York: Simon and Schuster.

Curwin, R. 1992. *Rediscovering hope: Our greatest teaching strategy.* Bloomington, IN: National Educational Service.

Curwin, R., & Mendler, A. (1997). *As tough as necessary: Countering violence, aggression, and hostility in our schools.* Alexandria, VA: Association for Supervision and Curriculum Development.

Dreikurs R., & Cassel, P. 1972. *Discipline without tears.* New York: Hawthorne.

Elam, S., Rose, L., & Gallup, A. (2000). 32d annual Phi Delta Kappan/Gallup poll. *Phi Delta Kappan, 75*(2), 137–152.

Ginott, H. 1972. *Teacher and child.* New York: Macmillan.

Glasser, W. 1969. *Schools without failure.* New York: Harper & Row.

———. 1986. *Control theory in the classroom.* New York: Harper & Row.

———. 1996. Then and now. The theory of choice. *Learning, 25*(3), 20–22.

———. 1998a. *The quality school: Managing students without coercion.* New York: HarperCollins.

———. 1998b. *The quality school teacher.* New York: HarperCollins.

Glasser, W., & Dotson, K. 1998. *Choice theory in the classroom.* New York: HarperCollins.

Gordon, T. 1989. *Discipline that works: Promoting self-discipline in children.* New York: Random House.

Jones, F. 2001. *Fredric Jones's Tools for Teaching.* Santa Cruz, CA: Fredric H. Jones & Associates.

Kohn, A. 1993. *Punished by rewards: The trouble with gold stars, incentive plans, A's, praise, and other bribes.* Boston: Houghton Mifflin.

———. 1996. *Beyond discipline: From compliance to community.* Alexandria, VA: Association for Supervision and Curriculum Development.

———. 1999. *The schools our children deserve: Moving beyond traditional classrooms and "tougher standards."* Boston: Houghton Mifflin.

Kyle, P., Kagan, S., & Scott, S. 2001. *Win-win discipline: Structures for all discipline problems.* San Clemente, CA: Kagan.

Nelsen, J., Lott L., & Glenn, H. 2000. *Positive discipline in the classroom.* Rocklin, CA: Prima.

Orlich, D., Harder, R., Callahan, R., & Gibson, H. (2000). *Teaching strategies: A guide to better instruction* (6th ed.). Boston: Houghton Mifflin.

Redl, F., & Wattenberg, W. 1951. *Mental hygiene in teaching.* New York: Harcourt, Brace & World.

Spence, G. 1995. *How to argue and win every time.* New York: St. Martin's.

Tully, M., & Chiu, L. 1998. Children's perceptions of the effectiveness of classroom discipline techniques. *Journal of Instructional Psychology, 25*(3), 189–198.

Weil, M., Calhoun, E., & Joyce, B. 2000. *Models of teaching* (6th ed.). Boston: Allyn & Bacon.

INDEX